EGYPTIAN PAINTINGS

Edward L. B. Terrace

OF THE
MIDDLE KINGDOM

THE TOMB OF DJEHUTY-NEKHT

George Braziller   /   New York

FOR

L.

Library of Congress Catalog Card Number: 68-31073

Book design by Thomson/Macek

Printed in Italy

PREFACE

The work which follows speaks for itself, but it is a welcome obligation to record my indebtedness to those from whom I have received assistance and encouragement. Professors Thomas O. Lambdin and George M. A. Hanfmann, my teachers for several years, instructed me in the fields of ancient language and ancient art. The interest of Mr. George Braziller, publisher of this volume, provided the inspiration for color reproductions of the highest fidelity. The transparencies from which the plates are reproduced were made by Creative Photographers of Boston under the direction of Mr. Mort Rabenow. Part of the costs of the volume have been defrayed by the Publication Fund of the Department of Egyptian Art in the Museum of Fine Arts, Boston. A grant from the American Research Center in Egypt, and leave from my own institution, enabled me to study many of the monuments in Egypt in 1967. Dr. Labib Habachi and Mr. Z. Misketian of Cairo were instrumental in the success of my work there. Mr. Horace L. Mayer gave me the opportunity to devote my entire attention to the manuscript for a short but vital time in 1966.

The extent of my debt to the pioneering studies of my teacher and colleague, Dr. William Stevenson Smith, is self-evident.

The work would never have been completed without the person to whom it is inscribed.

Edward L. B. Terrace
Museum of Fine Arts
Boston, November 1967

A Key to the Bibliography and Abbreviations

The sources referred to in the text, notes and descriptions of the plates are listed alphabetically in the section entitled Bibliography and Abbreviations at the back of the book.
The reader may also find useful the Chronology, which immediately precedes the Bibliography.

CONTENTS

LIST OF PLATES

9

INTRODUCTION

This work is primarily an exposition of the remarkable paintings found on the outer coffin of an official of the Egyptian Middle Kingdom whose name was Djehuty-nekht, and whose tomb was located at Bersheh in Middle Egypt. The tomb was discovered in 1915 during excavations begun by George Andrew Reisner, Director of the Harvard University–Boston Museum of Fine Arts Expedition in Egypt from 1905 until his death in 1942. It was actually uncovered by Lyman Story, for a while one of Reisner's assistants, who was in charge of the work after Dr. Reisner returned to his camp at the Pyramids of Giza.

Not only had the coffin survived ancient plundering and fire, but it was nearly lost on its way to America. After it had been conceded to the Museum of Fine Arts in a division of finds with the Egyptian Service des Antiquités, it had to await the close of the First World War for shipment to Boston, and it was not until the end of 1920 that this could be effected. During transport on the vessel *Clan Murdoch,* a fire broke out in the ship and was extinguished only by the use of great quantities of water. As a result, many of the antiquities on board were damaged by water, but miraculously the delicate paintings of the coffin suffered almost no harm.

Djehuty-nekht, whose name means "Thoth is strong," was a nomarch or local prince of the Hare Nome in Middle Egypt, the titular deity of which was the ibis-god of truth and wisdom, Thoth in Greek, Djehuty in Egyptian. Like countless other men from ancient Egypt, we know nothing else about Djehuty-nekht. Neither the inscriptions on his two coffins, except for his name and two titles, nor any other source, so far as we know, tells us anything about him or his works. Nor do we know anything of his family, either forebears or progeny, except that his wife, buried in his chamber, had the same name as her husband. We assume she was his wife because husband and wife were customarily buried together, and not because of any specific reference in the coffin inscriptions.

It was within Djehuty-nekht's power to lend his patronage to one of the great masters of the art of painting. But the master of the coffin of Djehuty-nekht is even more anonymous than his patron; neither his name nor any other work by him is known. Moreover, although other paintings in Middle Egypt approach those of the coffin in style, we cannot attribute any of these to his hand. Yet the lack of identification is not in itself very significant. For an appreciation of a work of art, its antecedents, associations, and successors are not really so important. It is the object itself—namely its form, and perhaps its purpose—which speaks to us; and that is all we need. On the other hand, one reason for our immediate comprehension of the Djehuty-nekht paintings as the great works they are, is our knowledge of earlier and later Middle Kingdom painting. Thus, I have tried to place the paintings in context in Chapter V.

I am not a philologist and, therefore, have not dealt at all with the inscriptions, except

10

to mention an occasional word because of some special interest of its signs. The inscriptions are of two kinds, the larger number of them being the impenetrable Coffin Texts, spells of various kinds devoted to the well-being of the deceased in the afterlife.[1] Most of these are incised on all sides of the coffin. The other inscriptions are the so-called *ḥtp-di-nsw*-formula, rendered by the eminent Egyptologist Gardiner as "A boon which the king gives. . . ." In earlier periods the king together with a deity or deities made his presentation of offerings and assurances of well-being to the deceased, but by the Middle Kingdom, the king made offerings to a god, that the latter might bestow them on the deceased.[2]

In concentrating on form and color as two of the essential aspects—if not *the* essential aspects—of the aesthetic principle, I follow the precept set down by Henri Frankfort in his penetrating essay "On Egyptian Art."[3] If in taking this "preliminary stage"[4] my analysis is found to be wanting in other respects, I can only argue that these aesthetic aspects are as essential to an understanding of the coffin as any other.

I do not claim that this method will yield much greater insight into the Egyptian mind than what we have already (and it is little enough). My aim is simply to present a masterpiece of ancient art which in many ways must remain remote from complete apprehension. I shall be satisfied if others will accept it at face value; that they, with me, will let their eyes wander from one detail to another and let the joys of visual perception be the simulacrum of the fuller comprehension we may never gain.

Ashton Sanborn of Cambridge, Massachusetts, served for many years as Secretary of the Museum of Fine Arts and, like Lyman Story, was for some time associated with Dr. Reisner in the field. Mr. Sanborn's account, made at my request in May 1966, is the only one we have from a person who viewed the coffins before their shipment to this country:

Late in the summer of 1920 I stayed for a short time at the Harvard Camp in Egypt before returning to Boston. One day Dr. Reisner called me into the courtyard where the cases containing the wooden coffins from El Bersheh were being assembled for shipment to America. "Come out here," he called, "if you want to see something beautiful." The cover had been removed from the heavy box containing the panel with the painted offering scene. The instant effect of this magnificent composition was startling. No painting that I have ever seen has made such a profound impression at first sight. The colors were as fresh and vibrant as if just laid on, and over the entire surface there was a delicate, pastel-like, powdery bloom like that on a ripe untouched grape. The memory of this brief sight of something so beautiful and so perfect created by a master nameless and unknown which by mere chance had survived inviolate through three millennia is fresh and clear and moving after more than forty years.

PLANS AND ILLUSTRATIONS OF THE EXCAVATION

Right,
Wadi Deir el Bersheh,
also called Wadi en-Nakhleh

Below,
The Boston Museum's
excavations at Bersheh

MAP OF THE
WADY DÊR EN-NAKHLEH
IN THE GEBEL EL BERSHEH.

*(From a Survey made by M. W. BLACKDEN and
G. W. FRASER, F.S.A., 1892.*

THE TOMBS AND QUARRIES ARE SHOWN IN FULL BLACK.

Scale of feet.

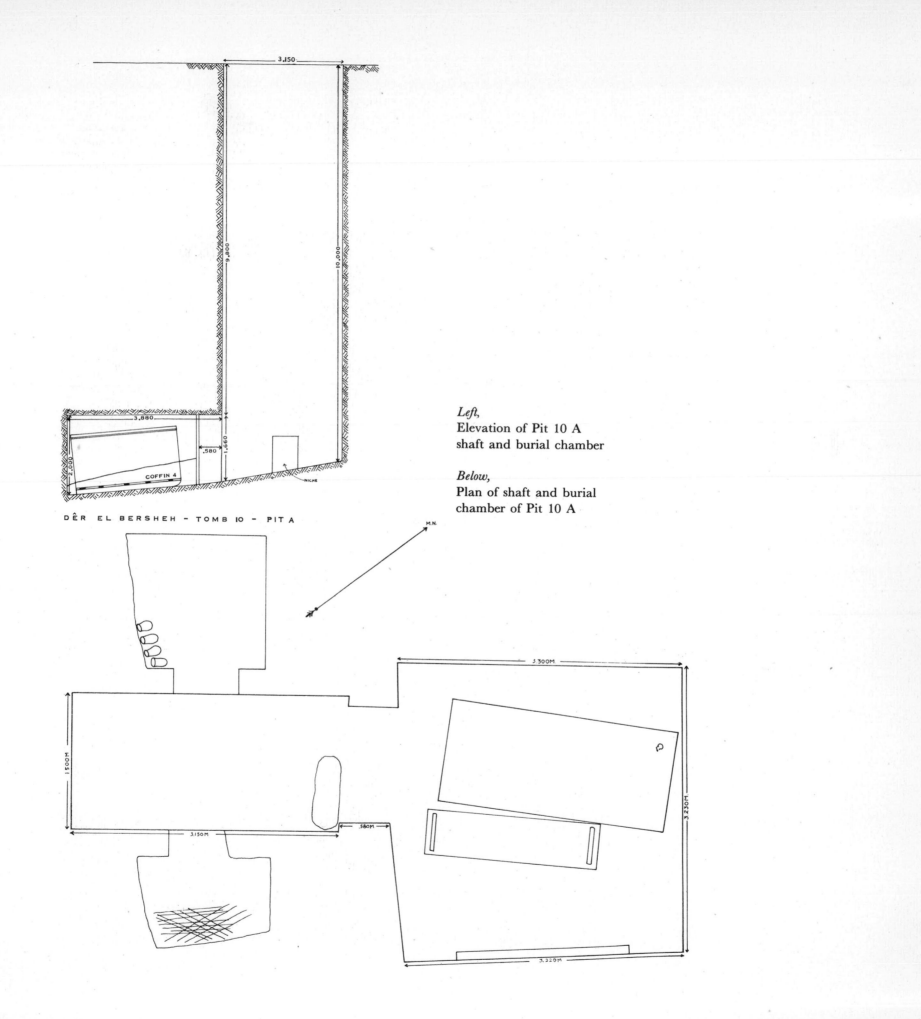

3,150

9,880

10,000

3,880

2,000

.580

1,660

COFFIN 4

NICHE

DÊR EL BERSHEH - TOMB 10 - PIT A

Left,
Elevation of Pit 10 A
shaft and burial chamber

Below,
Plan of shaft and burial
chamber of Pit 10 A

M.N.

3.300M

1.500M

3.150M

.580M

3.230M

3.220M

DÊR EL BERSHEH

1. *Above,* View of the northern side of the Wadi en-Nakhleh, showing the terrace of the major tombs of the Middle Kingdom (A 2202: This number refers to the negative in the archives of the Department of Egyptian Art, Museum of Fine Arts, Boston.)
2. *Below,* Area of the Middle Kingdom terrace including several exposed pits and lime stone debris covering site of Pit 10 A in upper left corner (B 2479)

14

3. *Above,* Mummy torso of Djehuty-nekht, thrown into a corner by the plunderers (C 6820)

4. *Above Right,* The coffins of Djehuty-nekht after removal of debris. Note beveled ends and rabbeting of lower edges for fitting to bottom. Also note dowel emplacements (C 6810)

5. *Right,* The sledge on which the coffins were first carried to and then lifted into the tomb (C 6804)

6. *Below,* Set of model tools from Pit 10 B, the pit located in the doorway of Djehuty-nekht's tomb (B 2569)

15

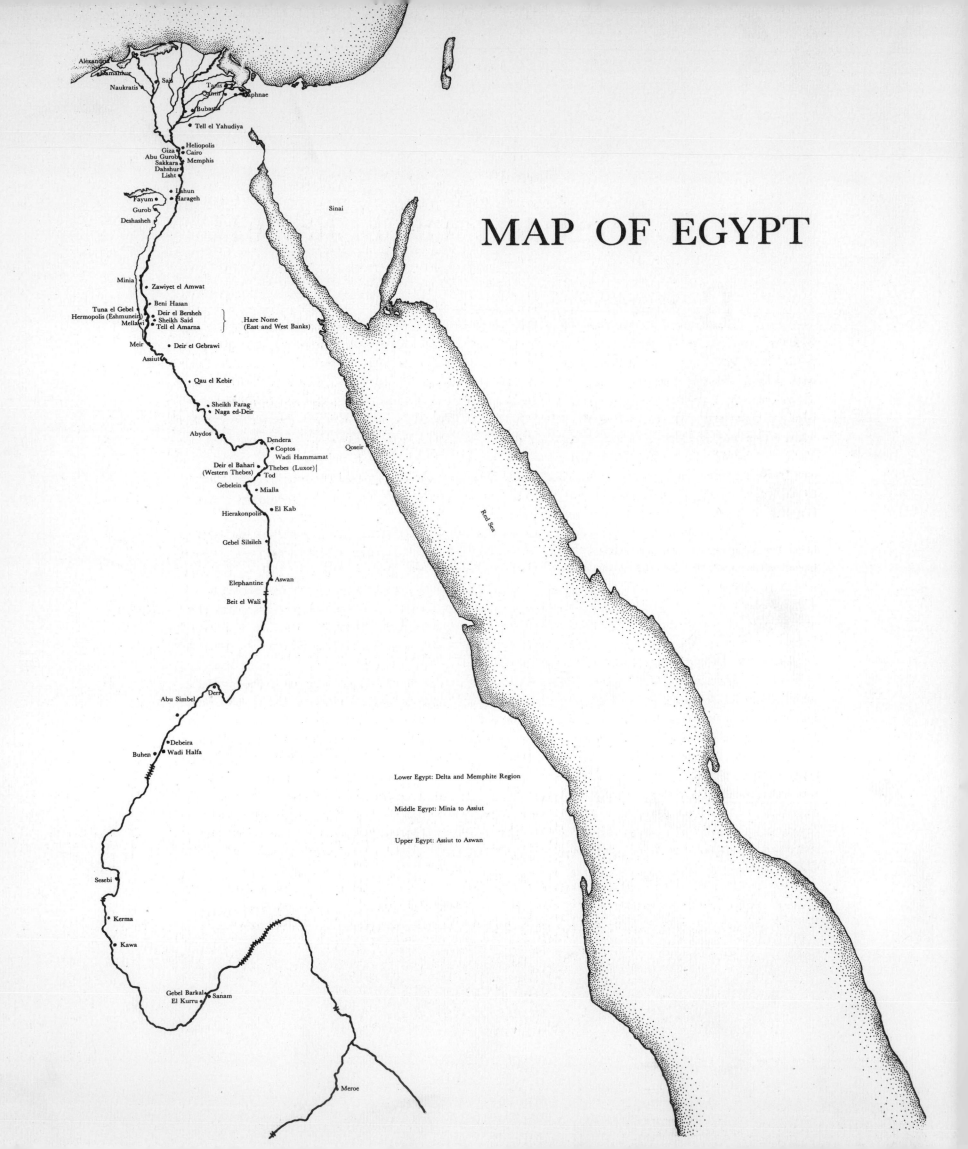

MAP OF EGYPT

Alexandria
Damanhur
Naukratis
Sais
Tanis
Qantir
Daphnae
Bubastis
Tell el Yahudiya
Heliopolis
Giza
Cairo
Abu Gurob
Sakkara
Memphis
Dahshur
Lisht
Lahun
Payum
Harageh
Gurob
Deshasheh

Sinai

Minia
Zawiyet el Amwat
Beni Hasan
Tuna el Gebel
Deir el Bersheh
Hermopolis (Eshmunein)
Sheikh Said
Hare Nome
Mellawi
Tell el Amarna
(East and West Banks)
Meir
Deir el Gebrawi
Assiut

Qau el Kebir

Sheikh Farag
Naga ed-Deir

Abydos
Dendera
Coptos
Wadi Hammamat
Qoseir
Deir el Bahari
Thebes (Luxor)
(Western Thebes)
Tod
Gebelein
Mialla
Hierakonpolis
El Kab

Gebel Silsileh

Red Sea

Elephantine
Aswan
Beit el Wali

Abu Simbel
Derr

Debeira
Buhen
Wadi Halfa

Lower Egypt: Delta and Memphite Region

Middle Egypt: Minia to Assiut

Upper Egypt: Assiut to Aswan

Sesebi

Kerma

Kawa

Gebel Barkal
El Kurru
Sanam

Meroe

THE HISTORY OF BERSHEH

Bersheh today consists of three large and flourishing villages: El Bersheh, Deir el Bersheh, and Nazlet el Bersheh. El Bersheh is the main place and nestles among fertile groves of palm trees and luxuriant plantations of orange and lemon trees. Deir el Bersheh, a Coptic village with a large Coptic cemetery of mud-brick domed tombs, lies just to the north across the fields and encroaches close upon the desert. Nazlet el Bersheh lies to the south and is the site of an extensive Moslem cemetery with its own variations of the domed tomb-chapels, which are frequently painted white. The wadi (a dry watercourse cutting a gap in the cliffs which line both sides of the Nile Valley) in which the tombs of the Middle Kingdom are located (Plan I, see pp. 12–13), almost due east of Deir el Bersheh, is sometimes called Wadi Deir en-Nakhleh (in 1967 the local people referred to the place as Wadi en-Nakhleh), but custom demands that we refer to the site as Wadi Deir el Bersheh or more simply and conveniently as Bersheh.

Probably there was always a tiny habitation at this remote place, if only a few huts to keep the attendants and guards of the nearby burial places. Whatever remnants of these ancient hovels there may be are no doubt to be found far beneath the present village of Deir el Bersheh, which is closest to the tomb sites and will remain hidden so long as the village site is inhabited. The ancient capital of the region is to be found at modern Eshmunein, which lies on the west bank of the Nile about seven miles in a straight northwesterly line from Bersheh. This city was called Hermopolis by the Greeks and by the Egyptians _Hmnw_ (most easily rendered as Khemenu), _Wnw,_ or _Pr Dhwty_ (_Per Djehuty:_ The House of Thoth, god of wisdom and writing).[1]

Hermopolis was the capital of what we call the Hare Nome, after its nome-standard, which features the kneeling hare as found in the hieroglyphic spelling of its name _Wnwt._ The name Hermopolis comes from the Greek equation of Hermes with Thoth, titular deity of the city. By the Fourth Dynasty the nome was already sufficiently important to warrant the superb schist triad found by the Harvard–Boston Expedition in the Valley Temple of the Mycerinus pyramid at Giza,[2] a triad representing the king, the goddess Hathor, and a female personification of the province, with the nome-standard on her head. The nomes were administrative districts during pharaonic times; probably some of them were originally prehistoric independent kingdoms or tribal groups of the shadowy period before the unification of the country by Menes. The more powerful often recouped their almost forgotten independence during periods of collapse of central authority, especially at the end of the Old Kingdom.

The Hare Nome lay between Beni Hasan to the north and Meir to the south. The burial place of its governors and nobles during the Old Kingdom was in the cliffs at Sheikh Said, south of Bersheh on the east bank of the river, and during the Middle Kingdom in the remote wadi just

17

east of Bersheh. In the First Intermediate Period there is a hint of an attempt to assert local independence from the Herakleopolitan and Theban rulers.[3] The nome's greatest moment was during the reign of Akhenaten when the heretic king established his new and short-lived capital on the east bank of the river, south of Bersheh and beyond Sheikh Said. At Bersheh itself, however, there is no record of this brief interlude. Presumably the principal reason for the Hare Nome's prominence was the location within its boundaries (in the desert behind Tell el Amarna) of the richest source of alabaster in Egypt: the quarries of Hat-nub which had been utilized from the Old Kingdom onward.[4]

Hermopolis was also the site of one of the three organized theologies in Egypt. The Hermopolite theology was based on an ogdoad—four male and four female deities—representing the characteristics of primordial chaos: "immense depth, endlessness, darkness and invisibility."[5] According to the cosmology of Hermopolis, the primordial hill—the beginning of the creation of the universe—first arose from the primeval waters here. One of the ogdoad of Hermopolis was the god Amen. For reasons unknown, Intef I of the Eleventh Dynasty introduced Amen into Thebes,[6] and when a Theban named Amenemhat—"Amen is in the forefront"—ousted the Eleventh Dynasty, Amen was made the chief god of Thebes and ultimately of the entire state, taking on aspects of the primary gods of the other cosmologies. Such syncretism was typical of Egyptian religion; if to some extent it was based on political opportunism, this syncretism nevertheless reflects a basic belief, or at least the will to believe, in the unity of religious experience. The ibis-god Thoth was not a member of the Hermopolite ogdoad and was named "Lord of Khemenu" first in the Middle Kingdom. The writing of _Hmnw_ signifies the ogdoad and might be rendered as something like "Town of the Eight."

As for Bersheh itself, it was already being used as a burial place in the latter part of the First Intermediate Period. Mastaba tombs discovered by Reisner in the plain near the mouth of the wadi belong to the Middle Kingdom.[7] The wadi was quarried in the New Kingdom and during the reign of Nectanebo (Dynasty 30, ca. 350 B.C.), and used again in the Roman period.[8] The site's subsequent history does not concern us here.

The modern discovery of the site of the Middle Kingdom tombs dates from 1817 when two Englishmen, Captain Mangles and Lieutenant Irby, on their return from a journey to the First Cataract, stopped at Raramun, a village somewhat north of Mallawi and opposite Deir el Bersheh, and with a local English businessman, a Mr. Brine, discovered the now famous tomb of Djehutyhetep. Theirs is the first modern account of the tomb: C. L. Irby and S. Mangles, _Travels in Egypt, Nubia, Syria and Asia Minor during the Years 1817 and 1818_ (London, 1823), p. 165. They were followed soon after by Bankes and Beechey, who had just succeeded, with Belzoni, in reopening the sand-covered entrance to Abu Simbel. Bankes' sketch of the famous scene of the hauling of Djehutyhetep's colossal statue was the first published illustration from the tomb: it appeared in Sir Gardner Wilkinson's _Manners and Customs of the Ancient Egyptians,_ edition of 1837, vol. III, p. 328. After this, a great many travelers and recorders visited the tomb: Rosellini, Bonomi and Arundale, Nestor l'Hôte, Wilkinson himself in 1841, Lepsius, and in 1889 a certain Major Brown who made a photograph of the scene of the colossus.[9] Of the other tombs at the site only Nestor l'Hôte copied several scenes in Newberry Tomb 5 (=Reisner Tomb 5) and Major Brown took some photographs in Newberry Tomb 8. Sayce apparently copied inscriptions in this Tomb 8.[10] Finally in 1891 Newberry and his party for the Egypt Exploration Fund arrived to make a survey of the site and copy what scenes

18

and inscriptions they could. In all they recorded ten tombs including Tomb 2, Djehuty-hetep. The results were published in two volumes, P. Newberry and F. Ll. Griffith, *El Bersheh* I–II (London [1896]).

In the following several years, the Egyptian Department of Antiquities made exploratory expeditions at the site.[11] The Harvard University–Boston Museum of Fine Arts Expedition, directed by George Andrew Reisner, reached the site on March 17, 1915, and left it on May 30, 1915. Fig. 1, p. 14, shows the main terrace of the Middle Kingdom tombs; Djehuty-hetep's tomb is at the far left of this upper terrace.

THE BOSTON MUSEUM'S
EXCAVATIONS AT BERSHEH

When the expedition came to Bersheh in March 1915, there was little to indicate a successful outcome of even the most extensive excavations. The main site had already been worked over and what remained was so encumbered with great rock falls, the result of earthquakes bringing down the limestone strata already weakened by ancient quarrying, that any further excavation appeared impossible. But Reisner had a nose for sites and Bersheh smelled good. Already in 1913 he had written to his friend Gardner Martin Lane, then President of the Museum of Fine Arts: "We will then go to another Middle Empire site in Middle Egypt, probably Bersheh . . ."[1] and in 1915, when writing to Lane's successor, Morris Gray, he said: "In 1911, I pointed out to Mr. Lane that we had practically no objects of the Middle Empire; and he urged me to make special efforts to fill the gap. Obedience to this desire took us to Kerma with the wonderful results you know and to Bersheh where we have just made a great 'find'."[2]

Kerma had indeed been a sensational site. It lay far to the south in the Sudan's Dongola province, and was found to have been a fortified trading center of the Middle Kingdom, with Old Kingdom antecedents and a subsequent habitation during the Hyksos Period. The material unearthed at this remote place revealed a rich local center where Egyptian skills flourished next to native crafts, the two frequently mingling, with astonishing results.[3] Many of the objects excavated at Kerma are now in the Museum of Fine Arts in Boston, and the most famous of these is the over life-size black granite statue of Sennuwy, lady of the fort's governor Hepdjefa during the reign of Sesostris I (1971–1928 B.C.), one of the finest female statues preserved from the Middle Kingdom.[4]

Although Reisner had obtained a concession for Bersheh in April 1913, it was not until March 1915 that he was able to make use of it, when he had completed the Kerma excavations and was returning north to Giza. He had with him as his assistant, Lyman Story, and his plan was to go to Bersheh with Story, make a brief survey with him, and then leave his assistant to complete a more or less clearing operation in the devastated area of the Middle Kingdom rock-cut tombs and also to examine the surrounding territory. The dry, precise entries by Reisner in the expedition diary do not obscure the romance, the reined-in excitement, of the settling in at a new site:

Wednesday, March 17 [*1915*]. Left at 6:30 A.M. for Mallawi [from Luxor]. Story stopped at Abydos. Arrived Mallawi at 3:47 P.M. Carriage to river; ferry; donkeys and camels to tents beside el Bersheh village. Fine sunset.
Thursday, March 18. Began examining ground to south. In the afternoon rode to Deir el Bersheh, the chief

20

site and examined the tombs on the north of the wadi, high up. Some pits open. Rest a mass of ransacked rubbish, limestone quarry debris. Impossible to see what has been cleared and what has not been cleared. Great damage done by ancient quarrying.

Friday, March 19. Shifted camp to Deir el Bersheh, pitched tents on hard flat island in middle of mouth of khor [dry stream bed].

Reisner stayed at Bersheh until April 6, when he left for Cairo with his family. Before his departure, he had surveyed the ground, begun the clearing of the limestone terrace in front of the Middle Kingdom rock-cut tombs, undertaken the excavation of Middle Kingdom mastaba tombs discovered in the plain between the wadi and the village, and cleared out some Roman burials with grave goods of poor quality.

Evidently Reisner considered the site to contain little of more than passing interest, otherwise he would not have left Story—who had had little experience—in charge of the work. Indeed, it is pretty obvious that Reisner now considered the work to be no more than a clearing operation. It is curious that nowhere in his notes and records is there any reference to the earlier excavations, except once when, on March 20, he made the following entry in the diary: "In the afternoon went up on the top of the northern cliff and saw the two pits cleared here by the Department of Antiquities."[5] Even more curious, perhaps, was his abstention from re-recording the famous tomb of Djehuty-hetep of the reign of Sesostris III. The Boston expedition did clear the terrace in front of this tomb and found several fragments of reliefs and paintings belonging to it. Some of these paintings are of particular relevance to the discussion of Middle Kingdom painting in Chapter V and are illustrated in this volume (Pls. XLIX–LI).[6] An unfortunate feature of the dig at Bersheh is that nobody had copies of the Newberry-Griffith volumes or the records of the Service excavations.[7] Story himself was perhaps unaware of the earlier work at the site.[8]

After Reisner's departure, Story continued the clearing of the terrace, high up on the north face of the wadi, under the most trying circumstances. The disorder of the scene must have been most baffling; he was forced to use dynamite blasts to dislodge the larger blocks of fallen limestone which littered the terrace. Then, too, it was the season of the Khamsin—the spring sandstorms—and the wind-driven sand often made work next to impossible. At one point, the men—the faithful Qufti who had worked under Reisner for nearly twenty years—refused to work any longer, saying it was impossible to excavate under such conditions. Later it was the heat which caused hardship, and by May 14 Story himself found it difficult to continue much longer.[9]

But by then one of the great masterpieces of Egyptian art—the painted outer coffin of the Nomarch Djehuty-nekht—had been discovered. Story's laconic entries in the diary[10] give little indication of the excitement that must have prevailed at that time:

Friday, April 23. [Beginning of work on Tomb 10.] Clearing white limestone debris from Tomb 10. This tomb is under the massive debris in back of Tomb No. 7.

Tuesday, April 27. Clearing limestone, flint and fine dark dirt debris from Pit A, Tomb No. 10. In debris a large number of figures from model boat; frags. of oars and spars from model boat; lower part of unfinished seated limestone statuette;[11] large pieces of fibre rope; one glazed steatite cylindrical bead and one oval carnelian bead.

Thursday, April 29. Clearing large flint and limestone debris from Pit A of Tomb 10. At the bottom of the pit in front of the chamber are a number of mud bricks. One closing block (right-hand) still in place; in place of the other is a heavy side for a large wooden coffin. A small surface at the top of the entrance to the chamber was cleared and Reis Said and I were lowered down into the chamber. One of the large inscribed coffins (that of the man) is intact with exception of one end which had been pulled out; the coffin of the lady has been pulled completely apart and her head carefully placed on top of the outer coffin. One side of her coffin, with a fine inscription, leans against the west wall and the rest of the coffin is scattered about, a great part of it being outside in the pit. The only other objects visible are a number of model boats and two alabaster jars. The chamber is half full of debris. A telegram was sent to Dr. Reisner.

Friday, April 30. Clearing limestone debris from Pit A of Tomb 10, around the massive planks from the coffin thrown out of the chamber.

Saturday, May 1. Dr. Reisner arrived from Cairo. In the ordinary course this is the day of rest for the men, but 19 of the older men worked, bringing up parts of the large coffin which had been thrown out of the chamber by plunderers, and finishing the work of clearing the limestone debris from the pit. [The following note was added by Reisner, signed and dated by him on May 1: "The outer coffin A [Djehuty-nekht's wife, also named Djehuty-nekht] was dragged out (after being broken up) into the shaft. The inner coffin was broken and left; also the mummy. The models were thrown over the coffin B [the coffin of the prince Djehuty-nekht]. Coffin B, the north end was broken open, both outer and inner cases—stones and parts of mummy visible through the opening."]

Sunday, May 2. [Entered by Reisner]. It will take a week or more to clear pit 10 A properly and it is very desirable 1) to clear away between Djehuty-hetep and number 13, 2) to find, if possible, one more pit with objects in view of the division with the Museum,[12] 3) to make certain of the desirability of continuing work here. I therefore cabled Dr. Fairbanks [Director of the Museum of Fine Arts]: "MUSART BOSTON MOST IMPORTANT CONTINUE WORK BERSHEH: STORY'S DEPARTURE MAY 26 UPSETS WHOLE PLAN. PLEASE RECONSIDER ORDER. Signed REISNER."

The plunderers started a fire in the entrance of chamber 10 A, as shown by the charred cloth, but it was stopped by falling debris before it gained any headway.

[Dr. Reisner left Bersheh on Monday, May 3, returning to Cairo.]

During the following six days the pit was carefully emptied. Besides the coffins—four altogether, an inner and outer case for each of the two burials (Djehuty-nekht and his wife)—many coarse but lively models of daily life had been installed in Djehuty-nekht's pit, as was the finest such model yet known, The Procession of Offering Bearers (see Pl. XLV). Finally on Thursday, May 13: "The work of clearing Chamber 10 A was completed . . ." and on Sunday, May 30: "Remaining boxes loaded on boat before daylight and after loading completed the boat left in the morning. . . ."

Originally the tomb should have consisted of an entrance portico and one or more rectangular chambers cut back into the living rock, with the burial shaft sunk in the floor of the innermost chamber. The decoration should have included scenes similar to those of Djehuty-hetep: on the right wall, the deceased hunting birds in the marshes with a kind of boomerang, and on the left, the deceased spearing fish. The inner room should have been decorated with the so-called scenes from daily life.

Fig. 2 shows the condition of the site of Tomb 10 during the excavation and the immediate area after excavation and clearing. The exposed pits are 6 A–C, 7, 8, 9, 13, and the entrance to Tomb 5 (=Newberry 5) is at the top, left of center (also see Plan II). The massive limestone blocks just to the left of Tomb 5 cover the site of Tomb 10, and the black hole in the upper left corner is the present entrance to the tomb. Under this debris the walls of the inner chamber are still preserved to a height of a little more than six feet (2 m.) in most places. Above this the earthquake has taken its toll either in the complete destruction of the walls or in severe damage to their surfaces. The ceiling was completely destroyed, the tomb now being covered by a massive shift of the limestone strata. The doorway is preserved intact and is exactly six feet high (1.83 m.), taking into account the somewhat uneven surface of the floor and top of the doorway. The state of these walls suggests that they were roughly dressed only and never smoothed down to take painted or sculptured decoration. Plan II shows that Story did not complete the plan of the outer chamber (if it be that and not a portico). This is because of the huge blocks of debris which still cover the area as shown in Fig. 2, a photograph made more than fifty years ago. In later times the walls of these tombs were quarried nearly to their foundations, and Fig. 2 reveals that many tombs were not spared even the foundations.

The Pit 10 B was sunk in the entrance portico or outer chamber of the Nomarch's tomb. The pit's occurrence in this location is the only evidence for an outer chamber, because such subsidiary pits were usually placed in already existing chambers rather than in exposed places. The misalignment of the pit suggests that it was a hurried afterthought, and it is possible that the lady named Sat-meket buried here was related to Djehuty-nekht. In any case, the decoration of her almost completely destroyed coffin is close to that of Djehuty-nekht and suggests that a close temporal connection existed between them (see Chapter V).

Neither the importance of his rank nor the power of his patronage is reflected in the size of Djehuty-nekht's tomb. The inner chamber is a mere 4.50 meters long and 3.00 meters wide; what little remains of the outer chamber is enough to show that it could not have been much grander (see Plan II). The great depth of the pit, 10.56 meters, is not unusual (cf. Plan III), nor is the small size of the burial chamber itself, which is hardly large enough to accommodate the two large coffins squeezed into it (see Plan IV).

When the preparation of the deceased for burial had been completed, the now mummified body was placed in the inner coffin, which had probably already been lowered into the heavy outer coffin. The outer coffin had been placed on a sledge (see Fig. 5). The carpenter probably used an adze like that shown in Pl. XX to form the upward-curving open ends, to ease the problem of hauling it from the plain up to the burial place. Inside the rock-cut chamber and presumably accompanied by much ceremony, the great load was let down into the shaft and pushed into its tight-fitting compartment. There is no way of knowing with what particular poignancy this scene might have been enacted: was Djehuty-nekht's wife one of the mourners or was she already in her coffin awaiting her husband's burial? It is unlikely that her coffin can have been placed in the chamber after that of her husband; it was on the west side farthest from the doorway which was effectively blocked once Djehuty-nekht's coffin was placed in the chamber. At this same time, the Procession of Offering Bearers (Pl. XLV) was certainly placed in the tomb, as were probably the much inferior models, although some of these, if not all, may have accompanied the wife's burial. The canopic chest and the various other equipment were placed in their allotted spaces and the doorway sealed. It was blocked first with mud-bricks on the inside and stone blocks on the outside.

If it had not already been done, the niches on the west and east side of the shaft itself were now filled with four mud-sealed jars on the east and a pile of reeds and several walking sticks on the west. These niches were probably sealed with mud-bricks. Finally the shaft was gradually filled with sand and debris from the surrounding terrace. The debris and "fine dark dirt" excavated in 1915 had of course fallen into the shaft after the plunderers had sacked the tomb.

When the excavators arrived at the bottom of the shaft, they found only one blocking-stone still in place, the others having been torn out by the plunderers. The rest of the doorway as found was blocked by one of the sides of the wife's outer coffin which had been torn apart by the plunderers in their haste to be finished with a gruesome job. Part of this coffin had been pulled out into the bottom of the shaft. In the debris at the entrance to the chamber were found scraps of charred mummy cloth and some other blackened items. Apparently the plunderers had tried to destroy by fire what they had left. Fortunately, lack of oxygen or drifting debris snuffed it out before it could take hold. Once the debris and blocking materials had been removed, the chaotic condition of the burial chamber could be seen. Torn lengths of linen mummy wrappings, limestone boulders, sundered planks of cedar, scraps of wooden models: all were haphazardly heaped together inside the chamber.

In all this chaos, the outer and inner coffins of Djehuty-nekht stood almost untouched. Only the head-end had been torn off by the plunderers in their search for the precious jewelry adorning the body. The coffin of Djehuty-nekht's wife, in the more constricted part of the chamber, was ruthlessly ripped apart in the search for treasure. What was found we shall never know. All that was left of the pathetic remains were the head of Djehuty-nekht's wife, found on top of the lid of his outer coffin, and the torso of Djehuty-nekht (see Fig. 3) tossed into the farthest corner behind his wife's coffin, and a few other scraps. A second torso was found—probably the wife's—charred by fire. Beside the coffins, canopic chest, and wooden models, only a few types of funerary equipment were left, but these included alabaster and faience vessels, several bits of faience and carnelian jewelry, a pile of arrow shafts and a few other odds and ends. The very considerable number of wooden models included boats of various kinds, some of them well-staffed with crews, model granaries, butcher shops, and the like. The next largest group of objects consisted of model jars, primarily of blue faience, but included examples in alabaster, mounted on wooden slabs probably representing offering tables. The only other items of note were faience beads from a collar or bracelet and two scarabs with floral patterns (Exp. Nos. 15–5–32, 33; 15–5–59, 60). Altogether, several hundred objects were removed from the burial chamber of Pit 10 A.

THE OFFICES OF DJEHUTY-NEKHT AND HIS WIFE

The title *ḥꜣty-ꜥ* (literally, "he who is in the forefront") designated the primary office held by the men who were the chief administrators of the crown in the provinces during the Middle Kingdom. It is translated conventionally as "nomarch" from the Greek for administrator of a nome (= province). In several places in the coffin inscriptions Djehuty-nekht is given this title without qualification and we may assume that he was indeed a nomarch of the Hare Nome.[13] Although the

24

title *ḥȝty-ꜥ* is almost always preceded by *rpꜥt,* "hereditary heir,"[14] this apparently honorific title was perhaps not thought to be sufficiently important to take up space on the limited confines of Djehuty-nekht's coffin. It may be that had his tomb been finished, Djehuty-nekht would have had listed the usual range of titles and epithets accumulated by his predecessors.[15] Since the tomb was both small and unfinished we may perhaps deduce that Djehuty-nekht held office for a short period only, probably following Djehuty-hetep. It is possible that in his short career he was not invested with the usual panoply of status.

Djehuty-nekht's only other title is mentioned twice (on the exterior of the left side of the outer coffin, Fig. 7; and on the exterior of the head-end of the outer coffin), and it was perhaps the most important office after that of nomarch itself: *ḥrp ns.ty,* literally, "The one who controls the two seats (or thrones)." What this means is unknown. In the Old Kingdom the title apparently had no priestly connotation, but at Bersheh it has been called a title of the high-priesthood of Thoth, an office held by the nomarch.[16] Djehuty-hetep, Djehuty-nekht's near contemporary, in fact twice lists the three offices in this order: nomarch, controller of the two seats, great one of the five (the priest of Thoth).[17] Elsewhere, throughout the Bersheh tombs, the *ḥrp ns.ty* occurs third in the order: hereditary heir, nomarch, controller of the two seats;[18] and most frequently occurs second in the order: nomarch, controller of the two seats, overseer of the *ḥm-nṯr*-priest.[19] From these occurrences we can still not glean a hint of the real meaning of the title, and the mere fact that it is listed with the priestly titles begs the question, since it always follows a political title. Of the two probable alternative possibilities, I think neither has a better chance of being more correct. The office may represent a political one, referring to the nomarch as the representative of the double-kingship of Upper and Lower Egypt, or it may as readily represent the religious role of the nomarch in his capacity as high priest of the functions in the temples, relative to the theological concept of kingship itself.

The lady Djehuty-nekht is given two titles or epithets only, those of *rpꜥt.t* and *ḫkrt nsw,* occurring several times in that order. The first, "hereditary heiress," is the feminine counterpart of *rpꜥt,* "hereditary heir," and the second is now translated "king's concubine." If, as is likely, the latter is merely an epithet of nobility, the old translation "royal ornament" may come closer to the truth of its meaning. Of course, the *droit de seigneur* implied by the more recent translation might still have held effect in a society as sophisticated as that of the later Middle Kingdom, and there is nothing to prove that this ancient concept of hospitality did not still have a real and explicit meaning. While it is possible that the epithet "king's concubine" might in much earlier times have reflected a policy of marrying off ladies from the royal court to provincial chieftains for political gain to the court, it is hardly likely that such is the case here.

. On the other hand, is it possible that the lady Djehuty-nekht was the dynastic connection between the office of nomarch in the Hare Nome and Djehuty-nekht, who claims so little in the way of office? The deference he showed in declining to use the title *rpꜥt* and his refusal to name any of his family in his otherwise elaborately inscribed coffin, may well reflect a humble origin and suggest that he reached his high post through both special ability and marriage with a more legitimate member of the family which had been providing heirs to the nomarchy since at least the Eleventh Dynasty, if not earlier.[20]

EGYPTIAN TOMB DECORATION AND ITS PURPOSE

THE EGYPTIAN VIEW OF DEATH

The Egyptian view of the world was centered around an ideal balance which is summed up by their own word *maat* (Egyptian, *mɜʿt*). *Maat* is truth, order, balance, the rightness of things.[1] The first order was that of nature and its phenomena: the regularity of the ebb and flow of the Nile flood; the tour of the sun through the sky, its disappearance at night and reappearance at dawn; the tranquility of the climate. The predictability of these phenomena was impressed deeply in the Egyptian's mind, and as a result he saw essentially a world of changelessness and continuity. The flood might run berserk one season, but if so it was only an interruption because it would resume its normal course and continue its regular flow. In the same way, the sun might disappear at night but its reappearance in the morning assured the Egyptian of its continuity.

The Egyptian's view of death was not far from his conception of the other phenomena. Thus death was not a change in the course of existence but an interruption, a temporary one which was merely a passing phase in the continuity of existence. Since any basic change, such as the destruction of the body of the deceased, would disrupt the balance and order of nature, elaborate precautions were taken to assure essential continuity. But it was not the Egyptian way to take a simplistic view, and so he saw the deceased as continuing to exist not in one form but in three. It is difficult, perhaps impossible, to say that any one of the three was more significant than the others. The aspect with which we are most familiar, at least in terms of reference, is the *Ka* (Eg., *kɜ*). The closest determination we can come to in regard to the *Ka* is that it was considered the "vital force" of the individual, perhaps even his "personality." The *Ka* was not separated from a man during his earthly life and it preserved the essential quality of the individual after the interruption of death. The *Ka* therefore logically resided in the tomb. Although the *Ka* was thus immaterial, it does not follow that the *Ka* did not require material sustenance, or at least sustenance with a material form. This need was the origin of the presentation of food offerings at the grave and tomb and ultimately the origin of the content of the reliefs and paintings in the tomb.

A more material aspect of the deceased's continued existence was the *Ba* (Eg., *bɜ*). The *Ba* was the Egyptian's ghost: it was a form which could be manifest to the living. From the New Kingdom onward it was usually represented as having the body of a bird and a human head. It is

26

not difficult to imagine this strange creature associating with the demons thought to inhabit the desert, such as were depicted occasionally during the Middle Kingdom, the most famous of which is the strange monster from Beni Hasan with a feline body, serpent-like neck, and wings.[2]

The third aspect of the deceased was his *Akh* (Eg., *ịḥ*), which means "to become a spirit." This aspect was the transfigured spirit which escaped mundane association and was seen as one of the stars of the firmament. In this unearthly realm the transfigured spirit dwelt in a kind of eternal reunion with its peers. Frankfort has put it this way:

> The conception of the dead as Akhu . . . incorporates them in the perennial cosmic order, it views them as partaking of eternity in the revolution of the stars around the pole of heaven.[3]

Initially, so far as we can tell, it was only the king who reaped the benefit of a continued existence after death, but gradually during the Old Kingdom first the great nobles of the court and then lesser people began to participate in the afterlife.[4] The rise of a belief in the possibility of survival for every man came with the disillusionment which followed the downfall of the established order at the end of the Old Kingdom. If ever a civilization experienced trauma, it was then. The vast funeral establishments at Giza, Abusir, Sakkara and elsewhere in the Memphite region, their costs, and their exemption from taxation led to a serious weakening of the economic base, and a burgeoning bureaucracy helped to bring about the disintegration of central authority. These, among others, were major material factors in the collapse of the Old Kingdom, but their psychological effects may be judged by the lamentations of a man writing in the Intermediate Period between the Old and Middle Kingdoms:

> The bowman is ready. The wrongdoer is everywhere. There is no man of yesterday. A man goes out to plough with his shield. . . . The robber is a possessor of riches. . . . He who possessed no property is now a man of wealth. . . . Every town says: let us suppress the powerful among us. . . . The children of princes are dashed against the walls . . .[5]

For centuries the Egyptians had had every reason to expect the continued order of things "for ever and ever," in their own terms. Now their world and their view of it had collapsed around them, leaving uncertainty where there had been confidence, discontinuity in place of continuity, chaos in place of order. In this situation it is hardly surprising that the Egyptian sought some new support for the most ingrained of his world-views, the continuity of existence. If, momentarily, the gods had suspended the continuity of the state, it was no reason to suppose that man himself could not still achieve an ultimate balance.

The source of renewed faith in the orderly progression of existence was the very ancient concept of the king as Horus who sat on the throne of his father Osiris. In this view, Osiris had been an ancient king, slain by his brother Seth in a contest for the throne. But in the end the son of Osiris, Horus, was adjudicated to be the legitimate successor. Since Osiris was the son of Geb, the earth, and Nut, the sky, he was divine and thus immortal; therefore, through death, he was resurrected. Every king who sat on the throne of Egypt was sitting in the place of Horus and so participated in the immortality of Horus' father. At death, the king-Horus joined his father-Osiris and indeed became Osiris. With the collapse of kingship in the Intermediate Period, the common man no longer had the king to guide him through earthly or unearthly life. And in this crisis, he could turn to Osiris—untouched by the earthly chaos—and through Osiris find his personal salvation. The analogy of Osiris' life, death, and resurrection soon became an identity and every man now had the possibility to become an Osiris.

THE DECORATION OF THE TOMBS

The format of the Middle Kingdom tombs followed, with some architectural variations, the types established during the Old Kingdom: that is, they were provided with a burial chamber at the bottom of a shaft and one or more rooms above for the presentation of offerings to the deceased.[6] The decoration of the coffins—now usually of wood—and the rooms of the superstructure was no idle choice. Indeed, our word decoration is misleading because the sculptures and paintings were instinct with an essential existence necessary to the well-being of the soul of the deceased, which was thought to reside in the tomb. The reliefs and paintings were decoration only insofar as they were responsive to an aesthetic instinct on the part of their creators, and in the extent to which they arouse aesthetic response in us, the viewers. The subjects are those which had been employed in the mastaba tombs of Giza and Sakkara: the deceased seated before a table of offerings (sometimes referred to as the funerary banquet); the deceased inspecting the activities of his estates, receiving and recording the produce of his estates, engaging in the hunt. Occasionally more specific and original subjects were represented, sometimes referring to actual events, which were of sufficient notability for the owner of the tomb to have them depicted on its walls. Such a case is that of the Nomarch Djehuty-hetep of Bersheh (Newberry Tomb 2). During his lifetime he had made for himself a colossal portrait statue in alabaster, and the enormous labor required to move it to its final position was sufficiently remarkable to warrant having the event recorded in great detail in his tomb. Within the framework of the classical subject matter there was ample room for other innovating detail and original observations.

Essentially, however, the subjects of these representations were confined to the preparation and presentation of offerings of foodstuffs and objects of daily life for the use of the deceased in the afterlife. However, we must be careful not to oversimplify. The representations should be understood not so much as magic but as "safeguards," in the same way that the reserve heads of the Fourth Dynasty and tomb statues at all times were thought to be repositories for the Ka should the mummy be destroyed. Thus it might be thought that the "vital force" of food offerings and equipment—all necessary to the well-being of the Ka—was transferred from pieces of actual equipment and offerings to the scenes on the walls and in the coffins, in the event that any of the former should be destroyed or missing. It is significant in this connection that one of the words for "food" and "sustenance" is kꜣw, the plural of kꜣ. But the special feature of the Egyptian's viewpoint is the multiplicity of avenues he might take toward a given goal, and it is not impossible to accept the paradox of a purely magical nature and a much more subtle spiritual one for these representations. In fact, there can be little doubt that the unsophisticated saw in them magic instead of theology.

The role of the wall and coffin decorations was, then, a most vital one. Their beginnings lay as far back as the Second Dynasty and took the simplest possible form: a roughly carved slab of

28

limestone bearing a representation of its owner seated before a table laden with loaves of bread, as well as a list of offerings. The slab was placed in a niche on the exterior of the crude-brick mastabas of this archaic period. From this simple beginning developed the great scenes in relief and painting of "daily life" of the later Old Kingdom and subsequent periods.

The decoration of the coffins of the Middle Kingdom was a reduction, a "shorthand," of the large wall scenes. Accommodated to the greatly restricted inner surfaces of the coffin, the representations resolve themselves into the offering scene (the deceased seated before the table piled with offerings) and lists and pictures of selected kinds of objects. The texts include, as pointed out in the Introduction, the *ḥtp di nsw* formulae and the so-called Coffin Texts. The latter, a series of spells meant to assure the well-being of the deceased in the afterlife, are derived from the Pyramid Texts of the Fifth and Sixth Dynasties. The Pyramid Texts originated in the belief that the king alone could find salvation in death. With the rise of Osireian theology, the texts were taken over by other than royal persons and, with the addition of new spells, were inscribed or written on the inner walls of the coffins.

The niche was an all-important feature retained throughout the history of the Egyptian tomb. The niche was the "False Door" or the "*Ka*-Door" through which the *Ka* might pass from its abode in the tomb, to receive the offerings placed in front of it. It is shown three-dimensionally in its most elaborate form as a series of stepped indentations, the central, often very narrow, groove being the passage through which the *Ka* might move. On the painted wooden coffins it is shown in more or less elaborate form. The example on the outer coffin of Djehuty-nekht is probably the most meticulously detailed of those known (see Pls. II, III). Thus, quite logically, the *Ka* was provided with passage within and without both coffin and tomb.

THE STYLE OF EGYPTIAN ART

With some idea, then, of the spiritual nature of the decoration of tombs and coffins, we can more easily understand the basis of the Egyptian style. The quality of Egyptian art that is most striking to us, whose eyes are trained to see according to the values first established in classical Greece, is the way in which figures and objects are represented in space. We may, in fact, put the statement negatively: in two-dimensional art the Egyptian artist does not involve figures in a spatial context as we know it. The Egyptian does not use perspective, and every figure exists primarily as an isolated phenomenon. There are certain formal principles which unite groups of figures: composition based on harmonies of line and form and relationships of activities. But the essential feature of two-dimensional art in Egypt is the exact definition of each figure and object as a separate entity made meaningful by the importance attached to it in its isolation. In the single figure itself, certain elements are considered essential to the proper "description" of it, whether it is a man or a stone vase. These elements are abstracted and rearranged in a harmonious manner according to the principle of "what is known to be present," not "what is seen." This method of representation, called *ideoplastic,* is in accordance with that ideal of a proper balance of things which forms the basis of Egyptian thought.

We may use as a simple analogy the Egyptian idea of death: life is known to exist and, despite death, to continue, even if unseen in concrete terms. In the same way, the human figure

29

is constructed two-dimensionally to show what is known to be present, even if *actually* unseen (I take as an example the standing figure, but the principles may be applied to the seated figure and figures in other more or less dynamic poses): the head is in profile but the eye is seen in frontal view; the torso is also in frontal view, but the breast which is in the direction of the figure's movement is always in profile. Between the torso and hip the aspect changes to profile again, continuing through the leg to the foot, which always shows the large toe "in front." The arms, hands, and fingers are disposed in such a way as to show their most characteristic aspects—in the case of the arms the profile, in the case of the fingers the full view of them grouped tightly together and usually from the top, while the thumb is almost always in profile. These elements are not haphazardly or willfully "stuck together" as a child without experience might draw them, but organized in a logical system of their own.

The real problem of Egyptian art, as in all art created free from Greek influence, is the ambiguity which exists between the viewer and the object viewed. Before the Greeks, and today among peoples untouched by Greek thought, man did not separate himself and the objects surrounding him. In the visual arts, this has led to the avoidance or ignorance of scientific perspective, that is, the rendering of a subject from a single viewpoint, with the resultant falling into place in an *actual* temporal and spatial way of all the elements of a "scene," whether of a single figure or a complex arrangement of different subjects.

Actuality as a goal in the representation of corporeality has certain origins, whether purely logical or purposive, but it depends ultimately on the Greek discovery of the "I-it" relationship of man and his environment, the discovery of man and his thought as a central locus around which objects and external circumstances fall into place. Since the seventh century B.C. we have been unable to avoid its use, whether positively or negatively. Without this momentous awareness of the logical differentiation between one man and another, between a man and his surroundings, it is not important or even desirable to employ perspective with its ruthless insistence on the single viewpoint as the source of visual experience. The pre-Greek system sees man and objects as being of equal importance, and distant views as significant as close ones. Thus the ambiguity which arises in our attempts to differentiate objects and viewpoints in Egyptian relief and painting is not the fault of the artist, but the fault of the viewer who, to see properly, must disregard the habit of looking from a single viewpoint and look instead from a multiplicity of approaches.

If we understand art to be man's attempt to control the chaos of phenomenological experience, to conceptualize this experience in concrete form, then we can see a very real rationality behind the style of Egyptian art, a rationality which also explains its apparent conservatism. That this control was imposed effectively at an early stage is the real answer to the charge of "conservatism" and "unimaginativeness" so often made against Egyptian art. To apprehend the effectiveness of definition in Egyptian art is to apprehend its true quality. Definition—the sorting out in visual terms of the essential and non-essential—is realized by the precise and continuous outline, the silhouette, and massive volume undisturbed by any baroque influences. The value of the surface itself requires ideoplastic means because to employ illusionary space is to break up the surface into something it is not. We may conclude, then, that actuality is not the goal of the Egyptian artist because it does not suit his purpose, which is in fact to transfix objects and to define them in a space which acts as a continuum of the basic changelessness of the objects depicted.

30

"Naturalism," as we know it, is thus out of place in Egyptian art. Nevertheless, although it may be a misnomer, it is a useful term in describing such subjects as will be discussed in the next two chapters which, in the Middle Kingdom, reveal the observation of nature occasionally translated directly into two-dimensional terms.

THE COFFINS
OF DJEHUTY-NEKHT

DEVELOPMENT OF THE MIDDLE KINGDOM COFFIN

The great stone coffins of the Old Kingdom were often elaborately decorated on the exterior with the so-called palace façade pattern, a series of recessed niches which is thought by some to imitate or at least reflect the niched brick walls of buildings and tombs of the Archaic Period, and by others to reflect matwork hung on the light structures of early times.[1] The sanctity of these early buildings, especially perhaps the tombs, was preserved in the exterior decoration of the coffins, although there was an increasing tendency to limit this decoration to a line of funerary inscriptions. As a rule the coffin interiors were undecorated. During the Sixth Dynasty, rectangular wooden coffins with funerary inscriptions on the outside came into use. The development of the simple wooden rectangular coffin may be attributed to the lessened importance of the coffin itself in view of the greatly expanded wall decoration within the tomb. A Sixth Dynasty burial chamber from Sakkara, shaped like a rectangular coffin, is decorated with painted reliefs of the foods and containers of funerary offerings, with lists of them inscribed above.[2] This chamber and others like it are perhaps the prototype of later developments in the decoration of coffins.

During the First Intermediate Period, when there was relatively little wall decoration, there are more and more cases of limiting exterior decoration to some lines of funerary inscription and using the inner walls of the now common wooden coffins to show increasingly elaborate offering groups as well as the Coffin Texts. The sacred eyes—through which the deceased was thought able to peer into the outer world—and sometimes the false door were still painted on the coffin's exterior. This development was very prominent in Lower and Middle Egypt where ties with Memphite tradition were still strong. On the other hand, in Upper Egypt another type of coffin was being developed, and in it we can see that the untutored provincial artists of those unsettled times were experimenting with the forms of decoration in an effort to determine the most suitable one. Thus a coffin from Gebelein depicts on one of its outer walls a typically crude offering scene taken directly from one of the stelae of the period: a servant or priestly attendant presents a brace of ducks to the large figure of the deceased, whose wife stands behind him and his son in front.[3] An outer side

32

of another coffin from Gebelein is illustrated with a butchering scene and a mummy lying on a bed, subjects otherwise reserved for the walls of the offering chambers of the tombs.[4] A third bears a typical Intermediate Period subject derived from wall and stele decoration: the owner leads his dog on a leash.[5]

Such scenes indicate clearly what had happened to art with the breakdown of the Old Kingdom. The general decline in craftsmanship was accompanied by increasing economic poverty, and relatively less patronage could be given even the poorer workmen who were now available to decorate the funerary monuments. It was cheaper and easier to restrict the necessary offering scenes to the coffin interior or a stela where, in immediate proximity to the remains of the deceased, the scenes had their greatest potency. Of course wall decoration in relief and painting was still executed, but within a much more limited scope. Its important bearing on the development of paintings in the Middle Kingdom will be seen in the next chapter.

In the Eleventh Dynasty there are two last great examples of the use of complex exterior decoration on coffins of the Middle Kingdom. These are the two large limestone coffins of the ladies Kawit and Aashyt of the court of Mentuhotep from Deir el Bahari. The scenes of hairdressing, filling of granaries, milking of cows, etc., are the kinds of subjects which are found in tomb painting and relief of the period. But the new use of decoration on the interior surfaces is adhered to even in the case of Aashyt's coffin which has painted offering scenes inside. By the Twelfth Dynasty the usual practice, with a few exceptions, is to restrict all the offering scenes to the interior, reserving some funerary texts, the sacred eyes and sometimes the false door to the exterior.[6]

CONSTRUCTION AND DECORATION OF DJEHUTY-NEKHT'S COFFINS

Altogether four coffins were installed in Djehuty-nekht's burial chamber: an inner and outer coffin each for the Nomarch and his wife. Although the decoration of the lady's coffin reaches the high standard typical of work at Bersheh, it is otherwise undistinguished and does not call for special comment in this volume. As noted already, the Nomarch's two coffins were intact when found, except that the head-ends had been ripped off by the plunderers. The lady's coffins were torn asunder by the thieves and the pieces lay haphazardly in and outside of the burial chamber.[7]

The coffins are made of great slabs of cedar of Lebanon (*Cedrus libani*) fitted together where necessary with wooden pegs and tenons. Occasionally breaks or flaws in the slabs were neatly trimmed and filled in with a carefully fitted piece attached with small pegs as may be seen in Pl. XII. The sides and ends were held together with dowels and copper bands passing through the beveled ends of the slabs, thus tying together the adjoining pieces (see Fig. 4). The lower edges of the sides and ends were rabbeted for fitting the bottom which was also tied to the other pieces with dowels and copper bands passed through the ends of the four enormous crosspieces to which the bottom was doweled. These crosspieces in turn rested on the sledge used to drag the coffin to its final resting place (see Fig. 5). Each lid has two crosspieces which, when in place, prevented the lid from slipping off the coffin. At each end of the lid are the remains of two cylindrical lugs used to lift the lid into place, after which they were sawn off.

THE OUTER COFFIN

As we have seen, the subject of the deceased sitting before a table of offerings was already being used on stelae of at least the Second Dynasty. By the Eleventh Dynasty it was used frequently on coffins, although not yet formalized, and awaited the Twelfth Dynasty before its standard form took shape. The subject as represented on Djehuty-nekht's coffin is not, therefore, unique as such. On the other hand, there is no other example so elaborate and complete or one treated with such a high degree of artistry. Nor were the painted inscriptions ever so carefully drawn and painted before. The school of artists which supplied the princes of the Hare Nome with their coffins was, in fact, more advanced than those at any of the other provincial sites, and the coffins from Bersheh are, generally speaking, of a higher quality than those from other sites, including even the capitals at Thebes and Lisht. Few examples of the painted details of these coffins have been published, but some samples of inscriptions[8] show the meticulous detail which was lavished on them by the Bersheh artists. The same attention was given to the scenes depicting the piles of food offerings and the objects of daily life. There is a degree of monumentality in these paintings, and especially in those of Djehuty-nekht, which owes much to the art of the tomb painter.

The exterior of each side of the coffins, except the bottom, bears a wide band of the *ḥtp-di-nsw* formula and on the left side is a pair of sacred eyes (the mummy was placed on its left side to peer through these magic eyes). The inscriptions were incised and then filled in with a blue pigment which has oxidized to the dark greenish blue now seen. The ground behind the inscriptions was painted white, which is not very well preserved. The sacred eyes have blue irises with the whites painted their natural color, the pupils being black. These inscriptions are reproduced in Figs. 7–8. It is to the painted scenes and inscriptions of the interior that the most lavish skill was applied. The descriptions of the plates record these scenes in detail, but here we may outline the general scheme. Only the foot-end and the bottom are not painted, but even these slabs are covered with tiny inscriptions of the Coffin Texts. Portions of these texts may be seen in the Plates: they were first written with the reed brush dipped in black paint and then incised somewhat carelessly. Their over-all neatness lies in the careful arrangement of each column and the consistency of proportion rather than in any special care given to individual signs.

The most spectacular painting occurs on the left side (Fig. 9 and Pls. I–XIV) in the Great Offering Scene, the climax of the intentions so piously and copiously expressed in the long funerary texts. At the top is a line of the *ḥtp-di-nsw* formula beginning at the left and ending at the right with the deceased's name and his title of nomarch. The decoration is then divided into two parts by a long vertical inscription extending to the lower edge. This inscription is a speech by the *ḥry-ḥb* or lector priest who invokes all offerings for Djehuty-nekht and his *Ka*. On the right are two lists of offerings—oils, food, perfumes and the like—with small kneeling figures presenting some of these items. Below this zone are columns of the incised Coffin Texts. On the left near the top are vertical rows of painted Coffin Texts and under these is a repetition in slightly different form of the *ḥtp-di-nsw* formulae, which invoke several deities. Below is the final presentation of the offerings of food and drink to Djehuty-nekht. Completely surrounding the seated Nomarch and the attendant who presents him with incense is a great pile of meats, vegetables, fowl, and vessels containing drinks of various kinds. Directly above the Nomarch are several lines, vertical and horizontal, of funerary

34

texts. Above and in front of the attendant is an inscription (Pl. VIII) reading *sḏ.t snw-nṯr n kȝw.k:* "burning incense for thy *Kas.*" At the far left is a spectacular portrayal of the false door, the most elaborately detailed representation yet discovered. All the slabs except the lid are bordered at the top and on the sides with a block pattern (Pl. II) and at the bottom with a red guide line (Pl. IV).

The right side of the coffin (Fig. 10 and Pls. XV–XXXI) is divided approximately in two horizontal halves. The lower half is devoted to incised Coffin Texts. The upper half is a remarkable display of the painter's attention to detail. There are four lines of inscription devoted to funerary texts, the lowest of which is filled with small hieroglyphs forming a double line of text (Pls. XXI–XXXI). Below these inscriptions is the *Frise des Objets,* the objects of daily life which were thought necessary for the deceased's use in the afterlife (Pls. XV–XX). These are objects other than the food and drink plentifully supplied on the left side. All the essentials are here: a bed, headrests, jewelry, weapons, clothing, writing materials, tools, and even a little more food and drink. Each item is painted with the greatest care, and the most meticulous detail is shown, especially in the mirror case and fan (Pl. XVII). The sides and top are bordered with the block pattern.

The lid (Fig. 11) is devoted entirely to inscriptions, but the many columns of Coffin Texts are enclosed at top and bottom by a band of painted *ḥtp-di-nsw* formulae so decorative that we may call them ornamental hieroglyphs (Pls. XXXII–XLIII). The head-end (Fig. 12 and Pl. XLIV) has lines of painted inscription above a band of various objects as well as jars containing sacred oils; below are more lines of Coffin Texts. The foot-end and the bottom bear only the incised Coffin Texts. However, in the very center of the bottom a small panel of inscription was painted in blue (now greenish blue), bordered by a block pattern of blue, white, and black within which, on the right, is a band of yellow, and on the bottom a band of blue. There are three horizontal lines of inscription, of which the third line is completely illegible, and in a fourth band is an offering table painted red. The inscription is very difficult to make out, but from photographs made at the time of excavation and from an examination of the original by Dows Dunham in 1965, the following traces were observed:

The inscription is a pious expression of Djehuty-nekht's future in his "beautiful burial," and once more gives only the title of nomarch.

On the beveled inner edges of the sides and ends are vertical inscriptions of a funerary character. These additional texts, first drawn and then carelessly incised, are difficult to read and photograph. Most of them are the speeches of goddesses.

Two of the tenons holding together the two main pieces of the right side are now partially exposed and on them may be seen portions of inscription in an angular form of hieratic (the cursive form of hieroglyphic script). Here again the signs were first drawn and then incised. Some years ago Dr. Henry Fischer called to my attention the existence of pegs from Middle Kingdom coffins, which were inscribed with bits of funerary formulae (e.g., MMA 27.3.59). He has since provided the clue to an understanding of inscription A below, which otherwise is most elusive. Lacau, *Sarcophages* I, p. 159 (CG 28065), gives the full inscription from a similar tenon, in which the "uniting" of the limbs of the deceased is mentioned. This refers to the possibility that the mummy might be broken up and the spell is provided to assure that the gods will remember to bring the parts back together again. All that is preserved in A is *dmḏ ꜥt*, "uniting limbs," although the first sign is more like the hieratic for *nbw*, "gold" (cf. Anthes, *Hatnub*, pl. 12, graffito 7). On tenon B the first sign looks like the hieratic for *w*, the quail chick, and the second is perhaps *m*, the owl, or *ꜣ*, the Egyptian vulture. It is otherwise incomprehensible.

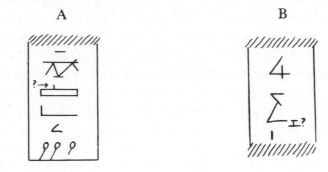

THE INNER COFFIN

Of the inner coffin we have to consider one detail only; in every other respect the workmanship and subjects are of ordinary quality. It is noteworthy, however, that a different technique is used for the major inscriptions. They were first cut out in sunk relief (in sunk relief the surface is left as the background and the relief is cut below the surface) and then painted, but not with the same refinement as on the outer coffin and obviously by a different hand. The one subject of special interest occurs on the right side of the inner coffin. Here we find the "Book of the Two Ways," a new development of the Middle Kingdom funerary texts. Its contents are a guide for the *Ka* in the Underworld, and, exceptionally, some coffins of the period are provided with a map of this Underworld[9]—such is the case here (Fig. 13). The color of the "Two Ways" themselves has disappeared, but the present discoloration suggests that it was originally red. The lower road is by land and the upper route by water, passing by hills rising from the waters. It recalls the Hermopolite cosmology which told that the primordial hill first rose from the inundation at Hermopolis. No one who has passed through the Delta, where great hills of yellow sand rise ponderously from the watery vegetation, can escape the awe which must have struck the ancient inhabitants of the Nile when confronted with the miracle of land appearing out of the water. "Lakes of fire and places guarded by fearful demons"[10] must be negotiated to reach the Fields of Reeds and Offerings where the deceased might spend his happy afterlife. In this representation the islands are depicted in white, labeled in hieratic written in black ink. The longer texts covering the map are crudely scratched in the wood.

TECHNIQUE AND PIGMENTS USED IN THE PAINTINGS

The paintings were executed primarily in natural earth pigments using gum or glue as a medium. The details of these materials are discussed below. The brushes used ranged from a rather broad one measuring about a quarter of an inch to an extremely fine one probably consisting of a single fiber. In Pharaonic times, brushes made of hair were not used; at least no examples have ever been found. Instead, brushes of vegetable fiber and wood were used. In the first case, the brushes were made by gathering together a bundle of fibers—including halfa grass and split palm leaves—doubling them over and binding together the upper part. A second type of brush was perhaps more common. These were made by taking various thicknesses of wood—in the case of the coarser brushes the mid-rib of date-palm branches—and bruising and fraying the end until stumpy bristles were formed.[11] For finer brushes the rush *Juncus maritimus* was used.[12] Such brushes or pens are often found in the scribes' palettes (see the palettes painted here, Pl. XVIII).

Ancient Egyptian pigments are almost invariably of earth or mineral origin, derived directly from the naturally occurring minerals or compounded from mineral substances.[13] Thus the usual red pigment was made by grinding to a fine powder the naturally occurring red iron oxides (anhydrous oxides of iron) and red ochres (hydrated oxides of iron).[14] Blue, on the other hand, although sometimes consisting of powdered blue azurite, was more commonly made from an artificial frit of which a copper compound (probably malachite, according to Lucas,[4] pp. 340–341) was the coloring agent. Fused with silica and calcium, the malachite is changed to a blue "calcium-copper silicate."[15] A more detailed analysis of the Bersheh pigments in the Technical Appendices to this book (pp. 167–169) confirms these findings.

Unfortunately, the question of the medium is as vexing here as it has always been. The usual vehicle for binding the paint to its surface was gelatine or animal glue, gum, and albumin (egg white). In nearly every instance of analysis very little of a definitive nature has been established because of the natural deterioration of these organic substances.[16] Such is the case with the Bersheh paintings. The surface of the wood gives the impression of having been prepared with some transparent size, but this material, if it exists, has not been isolated. We may now proceed with some general remarks about the colors of the coffin.[17]

Black: carbon, probably from charcoal.

Blue: in the two samples analyzed, the pigment was found to consist of the artificial frit called "Egyptian blue" (copper calcium silicate). The darker blue is probably the result of a higher percentage of copper in the frit.

Green: a mixture of Egyptian blue and the copper chloride compound atacamite, finely ground. Atacamite has not hitherto been observed in Egyptian pigments. Recently an examination of some pigments from the Procession (Pl. XLV) revealed that the green used on the mirror case is also atacamite.

Red: made from iron oxide (haematite), while the pink is a mixture of iron oxide with a high percentage of calcium carbonate. The darker reds contain some carbon.

White: calcium carbonate. On the fragment of another coffin from Pit 10 A the white is calcium sulphate (gypsum), of which there is a large quarry not far north of Bersheh.

Yellow: arsenic trisulfide (orpiment). Yellow is sometimes derived from yellow ochre (hydrated oxides of iron).

THE PAINTINGS

In the traditional style of Egyptian painting, *line* performs the all-important function of defining form, and in the Bersheh coffin the outline is still used occasionally for this purpose. Its use here is so refined that it has become calligraphic, as in the outline defining the foreparts of a lion in Pl. VI. The exceptional character of this and many other details is that the outline, when it was used, had been drawn *after* the colors were laid on. Usually the painter drew the outlines of his subjects, filling them in with color, or reinforced the outlines after coloring. The results are often stilted, lacking the spontaneity of free-hand drawing or painting directly without outline. It is true that much of the design of these paintings was drawn in preliminary outlines (usually red) and this can be detected occasionally. However, instead of following these original outlines rigidly and leaving them exposed, the master has almost invariably chosen to cover them completely with his colors and when he elected to use an outline he added it later, discreetly and selectively. The dove (Pl. VII), the form of which is a creation of coloristic effects, was in fact drawn first with a preliminary white outline. The color alone proves that it was not meant to be seen, and very little trace of it can be seen. However, the original line of the curve from neck to breast shows that the painter found it unsatisfactory, and as he applied the white body color he drew his brush away from the original outline and gave the throat a more graceful line.

The line along the left edge of the dove's left wing may represent shading, as is the case with the hazy grey line separating the Nomarch's legs (Pl. VIII). Furthermore, other lines as used on the figure of the Nomarch indicate that the artist was aware of shadow and chose deliberately to represent it in his painting. These extraordinary examples are: the lines of dark red over the left shoulder, along the outline of the torso (stopping at the lower edge of the breast), down the inner line of the right arm where it was brushed over a thin black outline, and along the outer edge of the upper right arm. In addition to these details, there is the evidence of the contrast between the legs. The right leg is painted the usual red, whereas the left leg, partially hidden by the right one, is a darker red, exactly as if it lies in the shadow of the forward leg. Elsewhere, a thin black outline, applied on top of the body color, is very sparingly used: around the chin and throat and across the upper part of the left shoulder and forearm, from the nipple up to the armpit, around

38

the whole of the right shoulder and the lower edge of this forearm, as well as the entire right hand (unlike the left hand of which the thumb only is completely outlined).

It is difficult to say what the artist had in mind when he alternated the thin black outline with the broader, less precisely drawn dark red line. If the latter does represent an attempt to suggest the existence of the figure in space rather than separated from it, then we may perhaps conclude that the painter, having no scientific knowledge of such a concept, was unable to carry through to its logical consequences. Thus, the use of the black outline may represent the mingling of traditional habits with the experimentation of the dark red lines.

That these apparently minor details are more than fortuitous is shown by the treatment of the dove (Pl. VII), the ducks (Pl. VI), the onions (Pl. V), and numerous more minor items elsewhere which are noted in the captions to the Plates. The treatment of the dove is more exceptional than that of any other figure in the paintings. As already noted, the outline was first drawn in white, and then filled in with white pigment. After the base color had been applied, the breast, side (?), right (to the viewer) joint, and perhaps right wing were washed in pink with an orange-like tint. Ignoring the fact that he had, or would have painted two upswept wings, the painter then marked out in grey and black the scaled feathers and pin-feathers of a wing closed against the body. Then a darker pink (its darker hue is perhaps caused by its being laid in part over the grey and black) was daubed around each of the scales; the grey-washed pin-feathers were herring-boned in black line. The tail-feathers, solid white underneath, were sketched in with black around the outline and with grey for the inner feathers. These inner tail-feathers terminate in drops of black. They were then very lightly hatched in grey. The two spread wings (which were incongruously added) are contrasted realistically by showing the outer feathers of the left wing and the pink-hued fine feathers of the underside of the right wing. It is not certain if the left wing was entirely laid out first in white. Probably it was, but all that can be seen now are the first sketches in white of the pin-feathers. The underside of the right wing was very lightly scaled in pink over white; the pin-feathers, black at the tip of the wing, become greyer as they diminish toward the body. Although the forward wing is certainly meant to overlap the pin-feathers of the right wing, the effect is spoiled by the drops of black at the tips of these feathers. This heavy black is probably the result of stopping the brush and hesitating a moment before lifting it from the board. It must also be noted that one may distinguish the left from the right leg because the pink wash on the body continues through the thigh.

The remarkable result of all these details is an opalescence which is unique in Egyptian painting. Having observed the play of light on the plumage of a dove as it occurs in nature, the painter has succeeded in reproducing this effect with principles similar to those used in nineteenth-century Impressionism. This discovery was purely intuitive and is not repeated elsewhere. The use of both line and color to create—or at least to suggest—three-dimensional form within the limitations of two dimensions was observed in the figure of the Nomarch (Pl. VIII) and is seen again in the ducks.

The calligraphic line which seems to describe the form of the entwined ducks of Pl. VI does not, in fact, exist; a close examination shows that with consummate brushwork, the painter first laid out the ducks in solid white. Where the outline is visible, it has been drawn over the color put down previously. This may be seen in the right leg of the left-hand duck, on which the red outline is drawn over the white and the grey and black cross-hatching. On the other hand, the talons were drawn in red before being stroked over in black. The same means were used to represent the pin-feathers of the wings of this duck. But here, instead of following precisely the thin red guide lines, the artist has left the upper edge of each red stroke exposed. Perhaps it is too much to assert that the effect is a deliberate opalescence like that of the dove's plumage. Rather, we may infer that having found the result close to the changes of color produced by light which he had already observed, the painter then concentrated on creating this quality in the coloring of the dove.

The figure of the Nomarch appears to prove that the master of the Bersheh coffin was aware of three-dimensional form and that he tried to reproduce it in the two dimensions available to him. The differentiation of the legs of the left-hand duck reinforces this conclusion. The black scale pattern of the side is continued on the joint of this leg, but the scales are much smaller and lighter in color as they proceed toward the leg. At the point where the thigh joins the body, the scales become confused and dissipate themselves into the lightest and most tentative of grey strokes. To the left of these shy strokes are scaled feathers; to the right is the white underside of the other leg. While the thigh of the leg is anatomically correct, the leg itself is reversed in position and appears to belong to a fowl facing in the opposite direction. This incongruity is an expected convention in Egyptian drawing.

In his attempt to represent the form of the twisted neck of the left-hand duck, the painter was only partially successful. The upperside of the neck is joined incongruously to the torso, and, in contrast, the throat is joined to the back. Although this problem was too great for him, the master has used both line and color to join the parts of the body organically, even if they are joined in the wrong place. The black used on the back of the neck is shaded into lighter and thinner brush strokes as it joins (wrongly) with the torso. More remarkable is the transition from the back to the throat, even if it does occur in the wrong place. The scales of the back feathers stop at a point just below the blemish on the background under the n-sign. A hooked curve swells inward at the left and diminishes toward the outer edge of the neck on the right. Inside the curve, between it and the outer edge of the neck, is a series of crescent-shaped strokes, the curve of the crescent facing toward the left. The strokes diminish rapidly in size as they approach the meeting place of the hooked curve and neck on the right. Whether deliberate or not, the effect is a plastically realized throat, the feathers of which gradually diminish as they pass over to the unseen side.

These details are inconsequential to the structure of the design, but they are basic to the visual excitement induced by the use of color as a form- and space-creating medium. The techniques used here bring us to a most important conclusion: the master of these paintings was experimenting with new methods which were unique for their time. We shall see in the next chapter that the painter worked in a climate favorable to these experiments, but even in the more monumental art of the tomb painter there is very little which achieves the same level of innovation. It is therefore all the more a pity that we have neither preliminary sketches nor any other work which might be attributed to the anonymous master of the Djehuty-nekht coffin.

The palette used in the paintings is extremely rich and varied; the different application of colors will be noted in the Plates but here we may call attention to two or three special features. At least four reds are used, sometimes two or more in the same sign or object. The most common is the earthy, rather orange-red characteristic of the color used in Egyptian art. It is the primary

40

hue used to color the figure of the Nomarch in Pl. VIII. To the right of the Nomarch may be seen a bright, almost cerise red which is used occasionally elsewhere. The copper blades in Pl. XX are dark brown-red, and pink is found throughout. Sometimes intermediary versions of these reds are seen, depending on whether more or less white was used with the red. The blue, when it has not oxidized to blue-green, is a particularly pure and clear color, as is the occasional green (especially in the Offering Scene). The yellow is transparent, and one or two varieties of ochre are found.

The white underpainting which is found nearly everywhere imparts to the colors a particular translucence and clarity. This technique, discovered and deliberately used from the Renaissance onward, was probably used on the coffin to compensate for the dark color of the wood. As light tones of grey were usually laid on stone walls before painting—to provide a clean and nonporous surface—the technique no doubt suggested itself as being appropriate for the coffin paintings.

A SURVEY OF PAINTING
IN THE
MIDDLE KINGDOM

The art of the First Intermediate Period used to be rejected as decadent, primitive, naive, and in other ways inferior to the great achievements of the Pyramid Age. The disintegration of established canons is the chief characteristic of art in the period between the Old and Middle Kingdoms. On the one hand, this disintegration was seen as a failure to continue the skill of the Old Kingdom artists, and, on the other, the products of the period were thought to be too crude to have influenced the art of later times. It is now possible to see that the breaking up of old canons and the rearrangement of traditional color patterns—often fanciful and highly imaginative in the Intermediate Period—provided the more highly skilled craftsmen of the Eleventh and Twelfth Dynasties with new alternatives and new inspiration. The artists of the Middle Kingdom looked back to their Memphite predecessors for formal inspiration, but without the experimentation which had taken place in the Intermediate Period it is probable that court art would have followed the dry and dusty path of archaism.

Before the Sixth Dynasty, decorated tombs of importance in the provincial centers were rare because of the concentration of administration at Memphis and the wish of the nobles and officials to be buried near the king. As the bureaucracy of administration increased during the Sixth Dynasty we find more and more decorated tombs of provincial officials. In the region nearest Memphis and as far south as Naga ed-Deir the influence of the court style is strong during the Sixth Dynasty, and in such tombs as those at Meir, Sheikh Said, Deir el Gebrawi, and elsewhere, one can hardly distinguish a difference between the style and subject matter of the local tombs and those at the Memphite cemeteries. Farther south one detects the waning of the court's influence.[2]

Although it has been said that the relief sculpture of the Sixth Dynasty "detaches itself sharply from the wall,"[3] its very boldness and flatness emphasize its integral relationship with the surface on which it is carved. The heavy shadow cast by a form in high relief makes the object or figure represented stand out, but at the same time it draws the eye to the surface behind the relief. This boldness can be observed even in the more refined treatment of royal reliefs such as those of Pepi II at Sakkara[4] and in the cruder, almost coarse handling of reliefs in such provincial tombs as those of Pepi-ankh-her-ib ("Pepi-ankh the Middle") at Meir (No. D2).[5] In the Fifth Dynasty we can already see a separation of styles, reflecting a certain weakening of Memphite influence. At Sheikh

42

Said, for example, the relief is smooth and urbane, with the registers full of activity and retaining a certain degree of modeling within the individual figures.[6] Somewhat farther north, at Zawiyet el Amwat (also called Zawiyet el Meitin), the relief has a sharper edge, the surfaces are flatter, and there is a curiously broad separation of space between the figures.[7] At Meir, most of the Sixth Dynasty tombs could as easily have been decorated at Memphis.[8]

The change of spatial relationships noted in the tomb of Ni-ankh-Pepi at Zawiyet el Amwat points the way to the disintegration of tightly controlled space, which is a notably characteristic feature of Intermediate Period design. By the same token, the crowded, clumsy figures in the tomb of Pepi-ankh-her-ib at Meir reflect the same attitude of disregard for the classical unities of space and form of the Old Kingdom.

In the tomb of Iby at Deir el Gebrawi we see suggestions of the painterly use of color which becomes the feature of the best work of Middle Egypt in the Middle Kingdom.[9] For example, in a scene showing the owner seated before an offering table (*Deir el Gebrawi,* pl. XIX), his right arm is separated from his body by a fine line of the white underpaint left exposed. Perhaps not exceptional as such, it is still striking that the painter preferred the greater subtlety of a white "space" rather than the more usual heavy red outline. In the same scene, the monkey under the chair is painted in a delicate and clear blue, and the sketchy brush strokes suggest the quality of fur. Nevertheless, the figure is outlined lightly in red, and the figs, despite the curving green lines which hint at their globular shape, are so heavily outlined in red that they appear as flat disks.[10]

On a nearby wall (*ibid.,* pl. XII left) a man is butchering a gazelle which is strung up on a "hieroglyph"-shaped tree, the transparent green of which is outlined in red. The back of the gazelle is orange-red and the body is white. The effect of form given here is almost accidental, since there is no transition from the broad stroke of orange-red to the white body. This change in the hue of red, the blue monkey, ducks with pink wings, and geese with orange-red backs (red is apparently laid over an ochre-yellow here, *ibid.,* pl. XIX), these are harbingers of a new, "unrealistic" use of color in the Intermediate Period. Another notable feature of this tomb is the elongation of the proportions of individual figures, which is in marked contrast to the compact, Memphite figures at Sheikh Said in the Fifth Dynasty and at Meir in the Sixth Dynasty.

The painting from Tomb 359 at Naga ed-Deir (Pl. XLVI)[11] gives a very clear picture of what happened to color usage in the Intermediate Period. Dated tentatively by Peck to the early Eighth Dynasty, and also by Smith to early in the Intermediate Period, it may be taken as a classic example of Intermediate Period painting with Memphite affiliations. The latter are recognized in the still well-proportioned figures (but note the inconsistency in size between the heifer and the ducks or geese) and in the titles of the owner (see Peck, pp. 23 ff.). The departure from tradition is seen at once in the strange, unreal coloration of the fowl with their blue backs, orangey-pink bellies, and yellow tails. Also notable is the scrupulous detailing of feathering in black and red (red spots on the bellies). This kind of mannerism is found also in the tomb of Ankhtifi at Mialla[12] which was decorated perhaps somewhat less than a hundred years later. Especially notable is Ankhtifi's catch of fish which, with their green and white bodies covered with all-over patterns of green, red, and ochre strokes, strike a bizarre note indeed. From this kind of mannered patterning, it was a small step to similar detailing in the Eleventh Dynasty.[13] Further strange uses of color occur in this tomb: one of the grey donkeys becomes almost purple, a red dog attacks an ochre gazelle, the hunters chase pink deer, a figure holds green ducks. Perhaps strangest of all is the scattering of figures almost aimlessly on the walls, within very generalized registers. Although the principal figures are as always larger in size than the subsidiary subjects, they are grotesquely so. The almost stippled black mottling of a butchered ox is related to the mannered cross-hatching of the fish. Other cattle here (including a white cow with red markings, some of which surround ochre centers), in the similarly dated tomb of Ity from Gebelein, now in the Turin Museum,[14] and in the curiously archaic Eleventh Dynasty tomb of Djar at Thebes,[15] are marked with splotches of color which, as Smith notes, "show the preference of the period for reducing the shapes to a series of patterns, an unrealistic formal approach . . . never completely eradicated as the Twelfth Dynasty turned to more naturalistic forms."[16] The same may be said of the general principles of design as well as of individual figures, and is a notable feature of the relatively sophisticated Naga ed-Deir Tomb 359.

At Bersheh only the shattered tomb of Aha-nekht (Newberry 5) gives an idea of the transition from the Old Kingdom to the Middle Kingdom. What little color can be seen now shows that rather harsh reds, greens, and blues were used. Despite some awkwardness in several figures, there is a certain balance of proportion and sureness of line which reveals the strength of tradition in this area which contributed so much to the art of the Middle Kingdom. In addition to such traditional subjects as dancing figures (*El Bersheh* II, pl. XIV; cf. *Deir el Gebrawi*, pl. X), there are others which were developed in the Intermediate Period, such as the fighting bulls (*El Bersheh* II, pl. XIV),[17] and the griffin and other strange beasts of *El Bersheh* II, pl. XVI. These fantasies were used at Beni Hasan to the north in the Middle Kingdom.

Also in Middle Egypt are two very fragmentary tombs of the Tenth Dynasty at Assiut, those of Khety and Tef-ib.[18] In the tomb of Khety is a famous scene of warriors carrying shields, which reminds us of the almost constant state of conflict between southern and northern cities during the later Intermediate Period. For our purposes it is remarkable that these figures are drawn with agility (the work is hardly relief; basically it is drawing with incised lines). The sureness of line and somewhat elongated proportions hark back to the Sixth Dynasty work at Deir el Gebrawi. In the adjacent tomb of Tef-ib, the bare remains of a painted figure show a skilled and refined hand at work.

From what little is known of painting and relief in Middle Egypt in the later Intermediate Period, we can only conclude that a strong tradition of able craftsmanship survived during the turmoil of the era. In view of developments in the area during the Twelfth Dynasty, it is apparent that the great painters of the time were probably local men with local traditions and not, as has been suggested,[19] craftsmen imported from the Memphite capital at Lisht by visiting nomarchs.

From the Eleventh Dynasty onward we are more plentifully supplied with monuments which show the development of painting. In Middle Egypt the primary evidence is at Beni Hasan, where most of the tombs of both Eleventh and Twelfth Dynasties were painted.[20] There is little variety among most of these tombs, and there is no real stylistic change between Eleventh and Twelfth Dynasty examples. There are the interminable wrestling scenes ("war-games," apparently a leftover from battle scenes and other warlike subjects of the Intermediate Period) in which lighter red men wrestle with darker red men, the two colors evidently reflecting merely the desire to separate the two figures. While the colors are more harmonious than those of the preceding period, simple reds, ochres, greens, blues, blacks and whites are placed next to each other in solid masses without gradations. The figures are drawn with a lack of grace and with an awkwardness which continues to the end of the work there later in the Twelfth Dynasty.

Drawn with greater felicity but painted with no more feeling for the subtleties of coloration is the painted interior of the coffin of Aashyt from the burials of the royal ladies of Neb-hepet-re Mentuhotep in his temple at Deir el Bahari. The exterior of the limestone coffin is carved with sensitivity, although its mannered quality has been called dry by some. The interior is painted with offering and presentation scenes which are remarkable for the brightness and freshness of the colors. But the colors, rich as some are (e.g., the deep chocolate brown used to represent the southern lady herself) and delicate though others may be (e.g., the fragile light green verging on turquoise of several gowns), are still straightforward and are blocked out in large masses.[21] However, there is a certain lightness in the color scheme which is enhanced by large areas of background surrounding the figures (a similar use of space is found in the reliefs of the exterior) and within individual figures themselves. For example, there are several gowns in which details of pattern, indicated in broad strokes, are laid directly on the background with much of the latter left exposed. Another proof of the use of color in terms of pattern is found in the one depiction of Aashyt's hair as green. With this coffin and the paintings described below, we have reached the period of Theban supremacy. It will be seen, with the exception of Beni Hasan, that all the examples come from Thebes.[22]

The same scheme of large masses of juxtaposed color is to be found in the nearly contemporary burial chamber of the vizier Khety.[23] This is a curious tomb. The passage leading to the inner chambers was lined with fine-grained limestone blocks of the best quality, on which scenes (including the hunt, among others) were carved in the highly accomplished and mannered style of the outer walls of the coffins of Kawit and Aashyt. The inner chamber, however, was decorated with reliefs crudely cut and shoddily painted. This work was so incompetently executed that it lacks even the freshness of a student's first efforts. The burial chamber, painted by a trained colorist totally lacking in imagination, has all the simplicity and straightforward quality of a child's coloring book.

We have already mentioned the archaic quality of Djar's Theban tomb. This tomb, executed in the reign of Neb-hepet-re Mentuhotep, "must have been decorated by an old-fashioned country painter."[24] The inexpertly drawn, humorous, almost caricature-like figures have a closer affinity to the Gebelein and Mialla paintings than to the courtly style of the Theban Eleventh Dynasty. The newly discovered tomb of a man named Intef is located in the Asasif at Thebes, not far from the tomb of Djar, and is dated in the reign of Neb-hepet-re Mentuhotep.[25] The drawing has much in common with those of the interior of Aashyt's coffin, although the figures tend to be heavier. The painting belongs to the school which preferred large masses of color presented in broadly defined patterns, as already described. The colors themselves, however, like those in Aashyt's coffin and Khety's burial chamber, have softened, while some individual details are treated with a new lightness and delicacy of touch which is bringing us closer to the spirit of Twelfth Dynasty art. The most remarkable feature of this tomb is the depiction of an embattled fortress, somewhere in the Middle East to judge from the costumes, against which a siege tower is placed.[26] Elsewhere, armed men are shown in boats, although it is not possible to determine whether the men are battling with an enemy on shore or afloat. The subject may have nothing to do with reality. It may be only a pious reference to a general quality of "fighting spirit" which had given the Intef who was the founder of the Eleventh Dynasty the authority to establish Theban supremacy in Egypt. Although the details seem too specific to make anything but the most explicit reference to actual events, we must not forget how earlier scenes were occasionally copied later and used as if referring to these more recent times. A case in point is that of Taharqa, the Kushite ruler of the seventh century B.C. who, in his Nubian temple at Kawa, had carved a scene of Libyan captives with the same names as those copied by Pepi II at Sakkara (Sixth Dynasty) from the Fifth Dynasty Abusir temple of Sahure[27]—and we are not certain that Sahure's representation was any more original than the others. The lack of inscriptions specifying the armed conflict in Intef's tomb may well be due to the pious, rather than actual, nature of these scenes.

As a last example of Theban painting of the Eleventh Dynasty, we may consider the tomb of Dagi.[28] Here too the basic scheme is one of large areas of simple color, but the colors are light and clear, and there is a certain flexibility in the use of brush strokes and combinations of colors. The heads of cattle which are being led through water are splotched alternately with red and blue, but here, unlike the Mialla painting, the effect is far more naturalistic and gives almost the impression of the natural texture of hair instead of a pattern of stipple marks. Bunches of grapes hanging from an arbor are made almost real with dashes of blue on a broken red background. The drawing of the figures has a certain grace, but some poses are awkward in the way the figures at Beni Hasan remain throughout the Twelfth Dynasty.

The famous tomb of Meket-re, whose models are the pride of the Metropolitan and Cairo Museums, was mostly destroyed, but a few fragments of inscriptions in painted relief show a highly sophisticated use of color, including a rich brown which is lighter than the dark chocolate used to represent the lady Aashyt.[29] The brown is sometimes painted over yellow which gives the color an added luster. In the feathering of some of the owl hieroglyphs, the extremely fine brush strokes go beyond the outline of the relief. These strokes have the effect of breaking up the color surface. The destruction of this tomb by ancient plunderers is a great loss to the history of Egyptian art.

The first king of the Twelfth Dynasty, Amenemhat I, apparently a vizier of the last king of the Eleventh Dynasty, moved the capital from southern Thebes to northern Itj-tawy, near modern Lisht and not far south of Memphis. Primarily a strategic move (it had always proved easier to control the entire country from the apex of the Delta), there was perhaps a family motive as well. The families of the Intefs and Mentuhoteps must still have survived, and must have always been willing to consider the possibilities of trying to regain the throne lost to them at the end of the Eleventh Dynasty. At Thebes there is only one more important tomb of the Middle Kingdom, that of the noble lady Senet who was wife of Intef-iker, a vizier of Sesostris I, second king of the Dynasty.[30] This tomb is highly interesting because it can hardly be distinguished from the best work of the Eleventh Dynasty. The faces of the dancing girls with their inelegant profiles and thick, strongly outlined lips (Davies, pl. XXIII) could as easily come from the coffin of Aashyt. Once again, the color scheme is one of large masses, one block of color after another arranged in a pleasing pattern. Like the colors of the Eleventh Dynasty, they have become more delicate: the blues are soft, the greens clear, the reds earthy, but the yellows tend toward strong ochre. In the hunting scene the rolling desert landscape is represented by a pink ground spotted with red dots. But the scene is organized in sharply defined registers hemmed in on either side by rigidly vertical nets, which are suitable to the precise, almost mannered drawing in the tomb (Davies, frontispiece). In a fragmentary scene which once

46

showed the king under a canopy or in a pavilion, the background is light blue on which, among other colors, a greyer and darker blue has been used. Elsewhere, the background is a rather yellowish grey. It is not difficult to find the origin of these subtle usages in the work of the preceding age, but we must turn elsewhere in Egypt for the full realization of their potentialities.

After the exception of the tomb of Senet, we can discuss the paintings of the Twelfth Dynasty reign by reign because the monuments come from a single region, that of Middle Egypt between Beni Hasan in the north and Qau el Kebir in the south. The only exceptions are the tombs at Aswan.[31] The first monument belongs to the reign of the first king of the Dynasty, Amenemhat I. The tomb is that of Senbi I (No. B 1, Senbi, son of Ukh-hetep) at Meir, and is not only the first great private tomb of the Twelfth Dynasty but one of the outstanding monuments of Egyptian art.[32] The decoration is entirely in painted relief. The relief is extremely low, carved directly in the living rock of the cliff into which the chamber is let. The delicacy of the workmanship is reminiscent of the best Memphite reliefs of the Fifth Dynasty, and the figure style and subject matter is in some degree reminiscent of Memphite work. These similarities have led to the supposition that the craftsmen actually came from Memphis. But the Sixth Dynasty tombs of the Pepi-ankhs at Meir, the quality of workmanship at Assiut in the Tenth Dynasty, and that of Aha-nekht at nearby Bersheh in the same period, raise the question whether the revival of Memphite-like work at Lisht in the north in the reign of Amenemhat I, and here at Meir in the same reign, may not rather be due to the presence in this area of a school of artists still preserving close connections with the past. Since the innovations of a painterly style stemmed from Middle Egypt, some additional weight is lent to this possibility.

The naturalism which has been observed in Senbi's tomb[33] is rather more constrained than might be thought. It is due more to the general vigor of the scenes than to a real "naturalism" as we know it. Details, however, show that the sculptor who directed and presumably executed much of the work had a broader vision than many. The hog-tied bull (*Meir* I, pl. XXX.2) spews blood from his mouth and nostrils, and he struggles vainly against the encircling ropes. A man who lashes together the legs of another bull (*Meir* I, pl. XXIX.3) hunches his shoulder as he strains to pull the ropes taut. Wiry, in truth scrawny, Beja herdsmen lead surprisingly fat cattle to the Nomarch (*Meir* I, pl. XXV.2, 3). The finest subject is the hunting scene (*Meir* I, pls. VI–VIII, XXIII–XXIV), in which the undulating round lines for the first time move away from the horizontal. (It must be observed, however, that one visual effect of the few diagonals is to emphasize the flat plane on which the figures are laid, and the lack of true space around the figures.) Another advance may be noted: the Nomarch, leaning forward while drawing his bow, aims his arrow into the penned area of the hunt, and thereby brings himself into the action, unlike Intef-iker who had stayed behind the pen.[34] The ground of these little hillocks is painted pale pink, and was originally covered with tiny dots of red. The lack of true space and specific time does not prevent appreciation of the liveliness of the various actions which are taking place.

It is in the painting of the reliefs that we find the most interesting and new developments. In the bird-hunting scene (*Meir* I, pl. XVI.2) there are two "levels" of water, the lower one apparently meant to be read "in front" of the group of marsh plants, and the upper register of water in which the papyrus skiff is floating in a more distant area. The nearer water is a bright, clear blue; the more distant is greyer. The plants, their stalks turning, twisting and crossing in the liveliest manner, are olive green; sometimes green is painted over yellow, sometimes yellow over green. Ducks here and elsewhere have bright blue legs and beaks. Their backs are greyer blue, which shades toward white on the bellies. The heads are light red. No outline is used. Throughout the tomb the colors are extremely light and clear, a special feature of the Meir paintings throughout the Twelfth Dynasty, and one which we shall see to be typical of the best painting at other sites in Middle Egypt.

In the next reign, that of Sesostris I, we have paintings at Meir, Bersheh, Beni Hasan, and Assiut. We have already discussed the Theban paintings of Senet of this reign, and have noted that these have affinities closer to the Eleventh Dynasty. It is apparent that the school of painters at Thebes during the Twelfth Dynasty was still training its students in the old methods and outlook of the Eleventh Dynasty. Similarly, the painters at Beni Hasan retained a provincialism which betokens a strong local independence in the Oryx Nome. The tomb of Amenemhat (No. 2)[35] of the reign of Sesostris I has a siege scene in which warriors attack a crenellated city tower, surely a holdover from some earlier time and not referring at all to a recent or actual event. The wrestlers above (*Beni Hasan* I, pl. XIV) seem as out of place as the battle scene and the armed foreigners in pl. XVI of the same volume. There are many examples of awkward poses, a mishandling of the problem of representing the movement of arms and shoulders (e.g., *Beni Hasan* I, pl. XVIII, especially the lowest register). The colors tend to be hard and have none of the lightness which is so characteristic at Meir and elsewhere, and as in the general usage of the Eleventh Dynasty, they are laid one against the other, and the outline is used constantly and heavily.

The first tomb of the Twelfth Dynasty at Bersheh also belongs to this reign, and, like the Beni Hasan tombs, betrays a considerable provincial quality which is surprising at this site. Newberry No. 1 is the tomb of a Djehuty-nekht (presumably an ancestor of our Djehuty-nekht). Figures are drawn with the curious awkwardness seen at Beni Hasan (*El Bersheh* II, frontispiece and pl. V); and an unpublished hunting scene (mentioned *El Bersheh* II, pp. 18–19) is as stiff as those of Amenemhat at Beni Hasan and Intef-iker at Thebes. By the same token, the tomb of Sarenput I at Aswan (No. 36) of this reign is similarly inelegant, although the typically Twelfth Dynasty elongated proportions are beginning to appear.[36]

A remarkable fragment of painting preserved in the tomb of the Nomarch Hepdjefa at Assiut shows that the skilled craftsmen of the Tenth Dynasty had somehow passed their attainments on to their successors.[37] Hepdjefa was a great official who was governor of the Egyptian trading post at Kerma, near the Third Cataract in the Sudan, as well as Nomarch of the Thirteenth Nome of Upper Egypt. Despite the grandeur of his tomb at Assiut he seems to have been buried with his wife at Kerma, from which comes the great statue of the lady Sennuwy mentioned already.[38] The fragment which shows a scene of boys picking figs in trees and goats nibbling at the leaves of other trees is drawn gracefully and surely. The positions of arms show none of that ungainliness which was noted elsewhere, and although an outline is used throughout, it is a fine line. The colors, such as are preserved, are clear and light and include a light red as well as a darker brown-red. Clear blues, yellows, and green are also used. The leaves of the trees are drawn with a delicate touch.

Contemporary with Hepdjefa of Assiut is Ukh-hetep I of Meir (No. B 2).[39] Like the tomb of Senbi (B 1) this is one of the great monuments of Egyptian art. The work is executed primarily in relief, not all of which was finished, and very little color is preserved. What is to be seen now shows the same cleanness and lightness that is typical of Meir. Although these scenes are not paintings and barely even colored, they are so important for the history of Middle Kingdom art that we must discuss briefly their innovating character. What is new is essentially the concept of space, which takes the form in some cases of large areas of empty background and in others the treatment of individual figures and their position in space: outstanding examples are the figures who carry bundles of papyrus in an almost cinematographic progression. In both standing and kneeling figures in this scene, the movements of the shoulders are treated in the most naturalistic fashion, and the sculptor has succeeded, where Khnum-hetep's painter failed, in conveying a proper view of the torso in profile with shoulders attached anatomically (*Meir* II, pl. XXVI). In this same scene the verism of the facial features and expressions is remarkable. Above the papyrus-bearers is a group of blind musicians whose movements are so tense with vigor that one expects the sounds to issue forth from the stone. Immediately to the right of the workers, a youth strains with a lashing on the end of a skiff. His shoulders are hunched together and a straining thigh muscle is realistically modeled. Since the hunting scene is unfinished, its present character may be more accidental than intended. There is no ground line under any of the three registers of animals. The lowest, it is true, rests in part on the dado line, above which the background has been partially cut away, but only the giraffe touches this line with all four feet; the others are above it. It may be that the sculptors or painters intended to complete the scene with undulating lines under each register. By the same token, Ukh-hetep draws his bow within the scene itself and not from behind a net, but here again one cannot be certain that such a division into sections wasn't intended. Nevertheless, the sense of continuity which is conveyed in the papyrus scene, which is nicely involved in the preceding boating scene by a standing old man, suggests that the spatial freedom of the hunting scene was deliberate.[40]

From the next reign, that of Amenemhat II, there is one tomb each at Aswan and Meir. At Aswan the last painted tomb occurs in this reign, the tomb of Sarenput II (No. 31).[41] The few figures still preserved reveal a clumsiness which does not improve very much on what had been done before at this site. At Meir, however, competent craftsmen decorated the tomb of Ukh-hetep II (No. B 4).[42] The scenes are largely in painted relief cut in plaster laid on the walls. Much of the plaster has fallen and the scenes are fragmentary, but enough remains to show that the craftsmen belonged to a talented school, although a less imaginative one than that of the earlier Senbi and Ukh-hetep. The subjects are standard offering processions and the preparations of offerings for the presentation. The painted details are finely executed and the colors continue the tradition of delicacy and clearness. The color reproduction (*Meir* III, pl. XXX) gives a very poor idea of the use of colors to indicate that the women have red hair. On a lighter brown-red background, dark but bright red-brown stripes have been laid, which produces not only a new hue but gives some impression of the texture of hair. In a scene showing the roasting of a whole beef over a bed of hot coals (poorly reproduced in *Meir* III, pl. XXXI) the coals are convincingly rendered in dark and light red on a white ground.

The only tomb dated in the reign of Sesostris II is that of Khnum-hetep at Beni Hasan (No. 3).[43] The paintings are justly famed for the elaborate scenes of agriculture and daily life, the hunt which includes fantastic beasts of the desert, the depiction of a caravan of Asiatics from Syria, and the bird-catching scene. Mrs. Davies has reproduced five scenes from the tomb in her *Ancient Egyptian Paintings* (pls. VII–XI), and these show well the peculiarities of the Beni Hasan painters. The plates have tended to give a misleading impression of what Middle Kingdom painting is like in general: these paintings from Beni Hasan are exceptional. Plate VII shows a scene of men picking figs while green-backed monkeys sit in the tree trying to take their due share. The principal impression we get from the grotesque positions of the shoulders of the men is one of artistic incompetence, but the painter's efforts must be recognized. He was trying to represent the shoulders in space, as seen by looking across them from front to back. He failed in this, as he failed in attempting to do the same with the breasts which are shown one slightly behind the other. Similarly, in pl. VIII the shoulders of two men attending oryxes, and in pl. XI the shoulders of a lyre-playing Syrian are treated in the same ungainly, but experimental way. The famous scene of birds sitting in an acacia tree has been likened to stuffed birds sitting on an artificial tree, despite the careful details of color and feathering. The caravan (*Beni Hasan* I, pl. XXXI; *Ancient Egyptian Paintings*, pls. X–XI) appears to be too specific to be a rehash of some memorable event of the past. It must have been observed by the painter himself. The paintings of Khnum-hetep are not only the best at Beni Hasan, they are also the last.

With the reign of Sesostris III we come to the climax of painting in the Twelfth Dynasty. During the reign three great masters were at work: on the tomb of Ukh-hetep III at Meir (No. C 1), the tomb of Djehuty-hetep at Bersheh (Newberry Tomb 2), and the coffin of Djehuty-nekht from Bersheh (Reisner Tomb 10 A). Each of these is a remarkable monument; and the most remarkable is the tomb of Ukh-hetep III.[44] Blackman called it "far more gorgeous than those of the previous princes (of Cusae)" (*Meir* I, p. 12), and we can only add that it is by far the most gorgeous tomb painting before the New Kingdom. To walk into the now sadly shattered chamber is to walk into a world of light and color unparalleled before the great paintings of the Eighteenth Dynasty.

Directly in front is the Nomarch hunting birds with the boomerang, on the right; on the left he spears fish. Turning to the right, one sees the Nomarch dressed in a brilliantly colored gown watching the bringing of the produce of his estates. All the work is executed in paint except for the kilts of the Nomarch in the two swamp scenes. The kilt on the right is covered with vertical rows of alternating *ankhs, djeds,* and *sa-* signs, modeled in white plaster relief. The background is covered with faint horizontal red lines. The left-hand kilt is pleated in white plaster relief (*Meir* VI, pl. XXXI 2, 3). Every detail of the scenes reveals the hand of a painter who reveled in the use of colors, and the only color of the Middle Kingdom palette missing are the browns, used very sparingly elsewhere. A case in point is red, of which five different hues are used. A rather rusty red is used for outlines and is especially characteristic in the deck of the left-hand boat. Dark brown-red is used for the dress of the girl kneeling on the deck and for that part of the Nomarch's leg which is shown under the transparent lower part of his skirt (*Meir* VI, pl. XXV 1). The uncovered lower leg is stippled in dark red on light red. Several of the fish have pink scales. An orange-red is used on the tails of fish on the south wall (*Meir* VI, pl. XXV 2). Elsewhere (*Meir* VI, pl. XXVIII 2), marsh plants growing from clear blue water are shown against a light grey background. The stalks are red and the undersides of the leaves are green, but the upper sides are light tan (our Plate XLVII). In the left part of this scene (complete in *Meir* VI, pl. XIII) a crane stands against the transparent green of the marsh plants. Its back is a very clear blue and its belly white with some stippling of dark and light red on the white. Just below are the leaves of marsh plants, the curling edges of which are stippled heavily in red; while the other parts are white with faint red stippling.

On the north wall the Nomarch wears a gown or cloak with a unique pattern (our Pl. XLVIII; *Meir* VI, pl. XVIII). On a white background the artist has painted green horizontal

50

stripes. The top of each stripe is outlined lightly in red with a thin green line immediately below it. Directly under this green line begins heavy green stippling which becomes lighter and lighter until the white background appears untouched. Then the system begins again. The two bottom outlines are grey because the painter has drawn the green lines over the red. Beneath the cloak falls the lower edge of a dark grey dress which is almost transparent; where it covers the legs, the legs are shown in dark brown-red. The uncovered parts of the legs are stippled in dark red on light.

These few examples, which could be repeated in all details of Ukh-hetep III's paintings, are in a sense the ultimate development of the breaking-up of traditional color patterns which first occurred in the Intermediate Period. Here the color itself is broken up, as if to let light in and as if it were understood that color is a function of light. If the reader has been skeptical up to this point about the "painterliness" of some Middle Kingdom paintings, he will surely find that quality in the paintings of Ukh-hetep III. Despite the fragmentary state of this monument today, the colors are as fresh and undimmed as the day when they were first laid on the wall.

The tomb of Djehuty-hetep at Bersheh has been famous since the early 19th century because of the scene showing his workmen hauling a colossal statue of the Nomarch of the Hare Nome.[45] Smith has pointed out how much more of the decoration is in the form of painting than is indicated in the original publication of the tomb.[46] Although the work does not show the same concern for breaking up colors as that found in Ukh-hetep III, the range of the palette and the refinement of line is paralleled only in the Meir tomb and in the painting of the Djehuty-nekht coffin. The tomb has been fully published by Newberry and commented on in detail by Smith.[47] Therefore our comments will be limited to the three fragments reproduced in our color Pls. XLIX–LI and originally published by Smith in black and white.

Plate XLIX shows a man picking up a stack of wheat sheaves to put on the pile behind him. It will be observed that the minute detailing of the ears of wheat is as precise as the treatment of the owl hieroglyph, among other details, throughout the Bersheh coffin. The slight shading on the throat and cheek of the donkey is also related to the Djehuty-nekht painter. Uncharacteristically, however, the view of the farmer's shoulders is drawn with no more facility than Khnum-hetep's workmen. But elsewhere in Djehuty-hetep's tomb such details are treated with much greater skill. In this Plate we see again the light, pure colors of the Middle Kingdom palette.

Plate L shows in the upper register two women winnowing wheat. Once more the detail of the lightly outlined grains brings to mind the precision found on the coffin. The crinkly hair of the workmen below is another of those touches of realism that one expects to find in the best work of the Twelfth Dynasty. The finely drawn silhouettes of these faces are no less graceful than those of Pl. VIII. The freedom with which the vine in Pl. LI grows over and around red supporting poles is not unlike the movement in the fragments of plants found in the offering scene in Pl. V. The yellow background dotted with red spots is, as Smith has noted, found elsewhere only in hunting scenes in a desert landscape, where the ground color is always pink.

It seems evident that the painter of the Djehuty-nekht coffin and the painter of Djehuty-hetep's tomb were near contemporaries. However, despite the closeness of drawing and palette, the two cannot have been the same. This is seen clearly in the treatment of the owl and snake hieroglyphs in Pl. L, which differs considerably in the minute inner details. The style is the same in the use of elongated proportions and in the fact of the precise detailing itself, but the methods differ. The same is true of the fragment of Sat-meket's coffin found in Pit 10 B, sunk in the mouth of Djehuty-nekht's tomb,[48] which is of about the same date as Djehuty-hetep's and Djehuty-nekht's. It would be interesting to know if Djehuty-hetep's painter learned from Djehuty-nekht's, or vice versa. Unfortunately, the nature of the miniature coffin paintings is too different from the monumental treatment of the wall paintings, and without an example of the latter from the hand of Djehuty-nekht's painter, we can never find the answer. It is interesting to note, on this score, that the registers in Djehuty-hetep's tomb tend to be small, thus bringing the scale of the wall paintings closer to that of the coffin—another point which brings the two works very close in time and inspiration.

The last dated example of Twelfth Dynasty painting significant to our purposes comes from the last important reign of the Dynasty. The tomb of Wah-ka II at Qau el Kebir was decorated in the reign of Amenemhat III and, like the tombs of Ukh-hetep III and Djehuty-hetep, is the last and best tomb at the site.[49] Very little indeed is preserved of the decoration and only the long inscription and procession of offerings high up on the north wall of the "Great Hall" is preserved with any clarity. What color can be seen is transparent and light. Petrie, *Antaeopolis,* pl. XXIV, shows a fragment of dancing girls drawn with a light and sinuous line. The details of dress, jewelry and other ornament suggest that the painter worked from the same inspiration which moved the painters of Ukh-hetep III, Djehuty-hetep and Djehuty-nekht. In the west side room (plan, PM V, p. 12) there is still to be seen under the grime a very beautiful fragment of painting (Petrie, *Antaeopolis,* pl. XXV)—three lithe girls catching birds which fly in and around leafy plants. The twisting stalks are light red, and the tiny, delicate leaves, looking like liquid drops of light, are the most transparent green. There is an exceptional similarity between these plants and the tiny sprig of droplike leaves on the right of our Plate V, a similarity so close that one might be tempted to see the same hand at work. There are other similarities, like the profiles of the figures (cf. *Antaeopolis,* pls. XXIII, XXIV, XXV, with the Plates in this volume), the detailing of the owl hieroglyph (*Antaeopolis,* pl. XXVI, extreme left edge of upper register), the matwork patterning of an offering table (*Antaeopolis,* pl. XXIII, lower). Unfortunately, one cannot do more than cite these close parallels from the drawings published. A minute scrutiny of the paintings themselves might well reveal that the two painters are the same. From what little I was able to see in the tomb during a short visit in 1967, I am convinced that the painters of the coffin and the tomb came, at least, from the same workshop.

With this fragment of a once great monument, painting in the Twelfth Dynasty to all intents and purposes stops. Up to the reign of Sesostris III the noble princes in the nomes had evidently attempted to retain a considerable degree of local independence and there are hints that Sesostris III made a successful effort to put an end to this state of affairs. On this score, it is significant that it is in his reign that the last important tombs were decorated at most sites, with the exception of Wah-ka II who was still able to command sufficient authority to decorate a superb tomb in the following reign. Essentially, however, with the reign of Sesostris III the best craftsmen moved to the court, or at least no longer practiced their skills in the provinces. In some way, however, their talents were preserved and were the basis of the new outburst of creative activity which took place at Thebes in the Eighteenth Dynasty, following the interregnum of the collapse of the Middle Kingdom and the Hyksos intervention in Egypt.

52

THE PLATES WITH COMMENTARIES

Reality is no longer the colour surface as a positively existing thing; reality is that semblance which is born of the separate flecks, strokes, and dots of colour . . .

H. Wölflin, Principles of Art History

I THE GREAT OFFERING SCENE

This splendid creation is the culmination of all the artistry and invention so lavishly devoted to the coffin of Djehuty-nekht. The rich colors and precise details of the ornamental hieroglyphs and rows of offerings elsewhere are as nothing compared to the climactic treatment of this final presentation of food offerings to the deceased prince. Despite its otherworldly origin and intent, the subject is man's world: the produce of his industry and endeavor and his observation of the nature surrounding him. Although most of the animals and fowl have been slain already and the fruits and vegetables pulled out of their plantations, there is such a liveliness in the cacophony of the forms and their colors, and an excitement in the apparent disorder of the great heaps of objects, that we seem to be looking into a miniature world of extraordinary life.

The scene is enclosed at the top and right sides by offering formulae and on the left by the uniquely detailed representation of the false door. At the bottom there is only a thin red guide line on which the lowest items of the pile of offerings are carefully squared. The details of the scene are described specifically in the following plates.

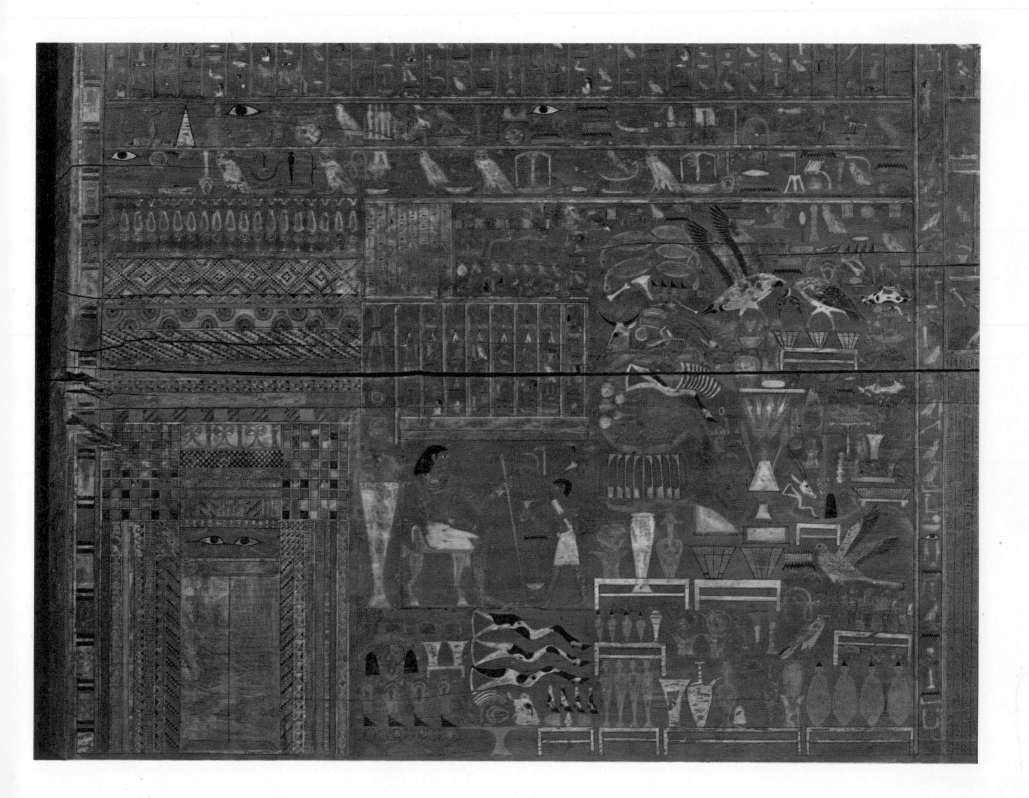

II THE LOWER PART OF THE FALSE DOOR

Like the rest of the coffin's decoration, the subject here is a perfectly conventional one. The elaborate patterning which surrounds the doorway itself originated presumably from rush or papyrus stalk constructions which were decorated with gaily colored matwork hangings and perhaps even fabrics. Nearly all the colors used elsewhere on the coffin may be found in the false door, even the powdery blue which is the feature of the ornamental hieroglyphs on the lid (Pl. XXXVII). Its use here may be limited to the vertical zone which is fourth on the left from the doorway, where it was laid in the center of red disks and has now almost disappeared. This convention was perhaps originally meant to represent the ends of papyrus clusters or rushes, but now it is geometric ornament only. A very delicate use of color is found in the zone of alternating chevrons and checkers above the eyes, especially in the tiny panel of vertical chevrons directly above the pupil of the right eye. On a white background chevrons of black, light and darker ochre, and red alternate. The lighter ochre may be the result of fading, but more likely the medium was a little thinner when the brush was dipped into it.

Nearly all of the design was first laid out in red outline, which was sometimes left exposed, as in the checkers on the right of the door, but usually covered over with whatever other color was required. In the case of the left-hand panel of checkers, the tiny red squares were painted over in black, much of which has rubbed off to reveal the double amount of labor. The doorways were first painted solidly with either white or ocherish yellow (it is uncertain whether the latter has faded to white or the white darkened in some places to yellow), and then made to imitate the graining of wood in red. Although the present appearance of the doorways gives the impression that they were washed with a light brown to effect the grain, this appearance is actually due to the deterioration of or possibly the soaking into the wood of the pigment.

The width of the false door is about .300 m.

III THE UPPER PART OF THE FALSE DOOR

The enlargement of this continuation of the false door provides an excellent illustration of the precision with which the outline of the design was laid out and the rapidity with which the painting was executed. The tufted ornament at the top is the so-called kheker frieze, thought by some to be "hooks" on which the mats and fabrics were hung (Vandier, *Manuel* IV, 41 ff.). The design must be derived from tufts of rushes bound together.

The richness of the palette is exemplified by the use of clear yellow against the white in the tuft of the kheker, but a light ochre on white in the "pod" below. The conventional nature of this use of colors may be seen in the large kheker on the far left, where an entirely different color scheme is used. The panel of alternating concentric semicircles is certainly derived from the ends of roof beams, whether of wood or a lighter material.

IV THE OFFERINGS

The apparent jumble of offerings is in fact a carefully controlled composition based on a vertical arrangement with occasional horizontal interruptions. Some details contrive to bring unity between the vertical zones, especially the curving forms of the great pile on the left which are echoed in the leftward diagonals in the central zone. The array of tables forms a transition from one rigid horizontal line of base to the freedom of the offerings above. The semicircle formed by the backs of the entwined ducks seems to reframe this horizontal basis and pulls together the three main vertical zones.

No kind of food and drink offering is missing from this abundant provision: meats, fowl, breads, figs, onions and a multitude of jars, presumably containing wines and beer and other unspecified liquids. Outside of the delightfully explicit rendering of each item, the most exciting visual experience of this scene is the rich display of color. Its great variety and the subtlety of individual details give life to a subject which is elsewhere stilted and conventional.

Above the five plucked ducklings the scribe has provided the specific label *ꜣpdw 5 wšn:* "five ducks whose necks have been wrung."

V THE ONIONS AND OTHER OFFERINGS

This plate shows the subtlety of color usage and the fineness of the drawing. The onions are washed with orange, imitating a natural appearance. The careful shading here seems to create a kind of false highlighting. Below the large bunch of onions is a basket made of green stalks bound together and containing figs. Above the onions, the section of ribs is curved in such a way as to suggest modeled form. Between the legs of the left duck is an alabaster bowl of lotuses, the stalks of the pads curving naturally. Two of the leaves of the branch curving to the left actually overlap one of these stalks and add thereby to the illusion of spatial depth suggested by the "highlighting" of the onions, the rendering of the ribs and the many other details.

These minute details stand side by side with the truly Egyptian way of seeing things. For example, the lovely stand of lotus blossoms and pods and the beautifully proportioned papyrus stalk, gracefully drawn as they are, consist of the silhouette only, as do the tables, jars, joints of meat, and most other things. Indeed, the lotus blossom is almost an artificial flower because of its being thrust into two cut-off stems, a fashion of forming bouquets still common in Egypt today. And nothing could be more artificial, more lacking in form, than the completely ideographic rendering of loaves of bread under the basket of figs.

The two single oryx heads are drawn in the same way, but with a uniquely refined line. The tiny sprig of dainty leaves is especially interesting because a similarly delicate treatment of leaves is found in two tomb paintings, one at the beginning and the other at the end of the Twelfth Dynasty (see Chapter V).

The label *ḥtpt* in the lower center is simply another word for offerings.

VI THE ENTWINED DUCKS

In Chapter IV we have already discussed the experiments with naturalism, which are found in the painting and drawing of the ducks. We need only add that this naturalism stands side by side with traditional methods of representation, seen in the hieroglyphs, the trussed carcasses, the table bearing baskets, the plucked ducklings. We may also repeat that the two ducks were not drawn in outline before painting. They were painted on in white first.

The tan of the trussed gazelle was laid over white underpainting which is allowed to show through at those points—rump, hind legs, underbelly, and front of the neck—where it may be observed in nature. To show the transition of shading between tan to the white belly, a stroke of yellow has been washed on. One of the cooking pots contains dead (white) coals, while the other has unburnt, live, and dead coals (black, red, white; cf. Pl. VIII). The pink hues of the wings of the right duck are due to the disappearance of the white underpainting, leaving the red outlines of the feathers to mingle with the red-brown wood. The somewhat yellowish cast of the heads of these ducks may be due to deterioration or oxidation of the original white. The spots of color on the body of the left duck are blemishes, and the ochre shading on the duck in the lower left is oxidation.

The inscription above the ducks reads:

n kꜣ · k ḥꜣ.t wḏḥw pḫr pdw stpt

"for thy *kꜣ*, the first (=best) of offerings, *pḫr*-offerings,

pdw-offerings, and *stpt*-offerings"

In his most helpful discussion with me about this inscription, Dr. M. Heerma van Voss of Leiden points out the likelihood that the *pḫr*-offerings are those carried by a butler "circulating around" a table, from the root meaning of *pḫr*, "to go around" and with the extended meaning "to serve." By the same token, *pdw*-offerings may be construed perhaps as offerings made from a "kneeling position," from the verb *pd*, "to kneel," a confusion of *pd*, "knee" and *pd*, "to stretch," as pointed out by Gardiner in *Gr.*[3] p. 566. Perhaps a simpler extended meaning is "offerings made with outstretched arms." The *stpt*-offerings, "pieces of meat," refer directly to the cut-up joints which are pictured below the label. (For these same offerings in Old Kingdom lists see Barta, *Opferliste,* p. 50, nos. 92–95.)

The trussed gazelle is labeled *gḥs,* "gazelle," and the lowest animal is described as *mꜣ-ḥḏ,* "oryx" (see the preceding plate). Directly over the intertwined necks of the ducks appears

the word *šn*. This spelling may be an unfinished or abbreviated form of *šns* in *šns dwiw i'w-r* or *šns dwiw šbw*, two more kinds of offerings (*Opferliste*, p. 48, nos. 19 and 25.) To the left, between the three dressed ducklings and the left-hand duck, is a further label: *ḥꜣ.ty*, "two *ḥꜣ.t*-birds." Normally the *ḥꜣ.t*-bird (perhaps a small bird of prey) is associated with Isis (see *Wb.* II f.8). Here the word refers obviously to the ducks, through some curious equivalence of *ḥꜣ.t* with birds in general, unless the word is actually *ḥꜣt*, "food (offering)" (see Faulkner, *Concise Dictionary*, p. 162). It would not be difficult for the scribe to confuse two different words which here stand for roughly the same thing: a food offering in the form of two birds. Although it is somewhat difficult to construe *šn* and *ḥꜣ.ty* together grammatically, there is no doubt of their ideographic connection.

VII THE DOVE

While the dove is a unique example of the use of color to create form (see Chapter IV), the Egyptian vulture (the hieroglyph *ꜣ, Gr.*[3], G 1) is a masterpiece of pure drawing. The colors are pretty but unmodulated. In the light feathers on the neck, we can almost see the hand of the master at work. These same feathery strokes embellish three hieroglyphs in the word *wꜣḥt* "oblations": the rope tied in a knot ⚭ (*wꜣ*, V 4), the twisted rope ⚮ (*ḥ*, V 28) and the swab made from a hank of fiber ⚯ (*wꜣḥ*, V 29). The loaves of bread on the table on the right were originally bright crimson, but most of the color has faded. An unusual olive-green is found in the ornamental base of the papyrus stalk which rests on a boat-shaped basket.

To prevent us from making an error in the species of the bird, the painter has labeled the dove *mnwt*, "dove." The first sign *mn* ▭ (Y 5) represents exactly its origin as a gaming board with squared spaces for the moves and the playing pieces lined up in a row along the upper edge.

Here we may see even more clearly the fine drawing of the head of the oryx.

VIII DJEHUTY-NEKHT

Djehuty-nekht sits holding a staff, while an attending figure holds out a footed dish of burning coals to him. The chair is the traditional one with legs imitating those of a lion. A rug or cushion has been thrown over the low back for greater comfort. The Nomarch wears a faience collar, the blue strands of which have oxided to a greener blue, as has happened frequently throughout these paintings. The yellowish tinge around the black pendants is due to a change from the original white. His two bracelets are made of blue, white, and yellow materials. The blue bands (the light powdery blue used sparingly elsewhere) are probably faience, but the white strands perhaps represent silver beads bound together with a gold button lock. The attending personage is sashed across the breast and wears his hair cut short. The yellow alabaster dish is heaped with burning and half-consumed coals from which a wisp of grey smoke escapes. The figure is about to drop a pellet of some green-colored material onto the coals. It is presumably the incense which is referred to in the inscription: *sdt sntr n kꜣw.k sp 2,* "burning incense for thy *Kas* two times." The determinative of the phrase *sdt sntr* is a kneeling figure pouring green pellets of incense from a *ḥes*-vase.

We have already pointed out the ways in which the master has tried to make the Nomarch a real figure existing in space (Chapter IV). Otherwise the figure follows the usual conventions: the torso in front view, with one breast in profile, the waist changing to profile, the feet seen from one view only. Although his left hand grips the staff correctly, the right hand is incorrectly placed. This has not prevented the painter from naturalistically drawing the cuticles, or from drawing a faint line across the back of the hand to indicate the finger joints. This line is at an angle which suggests, perhaps accidentally, a certain degree of perspective. The toes, although one is incorrectly placed, have nails curving over from the unseen side, a realistic detail found in many reliefs and paintings. The toe in the foreground curves upward very slightly in a clear display of asymmetry.

It is of some interest to note the sequence in which the figure of the Nomarch was painted. First it was drawn in red outline which was certainly meant to be hidden: in only one or two places can tiny traces of it be seen. Then a layer of white underpainting was put on. The jeweled collar was probably painted next, and finally the red body color. The sequence of red on white can be seen at the meeting of the kilt and the back of the knees at the front edge of the chair.

The curling smoke (its shape imitating the usual hieroglyphic form) was indicated first by a few lines of now hardly visible grey which were washed over with a grey so light that it takes on a violet hue against the red-brown wood.

Note that the scene is framed as a separate vignette, the dimensions of which are about .230 m. long by .220 m. high.

IX THE OFFERING FORMULAE (1)

The following six plates (Pls. IX–XIV) include most of the funerary inscriptions of the left side of the coffin. As explained in the Introduction, no attempt is made here to deal with these inscriptions in the form of translation and philological discussion. Their only interest for us is their illustration of an aesthetic motive or inspiration. Since most of the hieroglyphic signs are more interestingly treated in the larger hieroglyphs of the lid and right side, very little comment is called for here except to point out, from time to time, especially notable details. The plates run from the left edge to the right, in the order of the inscription, and conclude with two details of the list of offerings on the right portion of the side.

Although conventional in every respect, the signs of the inscriptions are rendered with a grace that belies the rapidity with which they were painted and written. In many cases, especially where they might have been most helpful to guide the brush, outlines were ignored. Thus, in the row of parallel vertical texts, which list various deities, the ducks in the fifth and sixth columns stand out as beautiful examples of pure brushwork, each individually worked and with different pigments. The man leaning forward on a staff (which has disappeared) at the bottom of this same sixth column is another pretty piece of free brushwork. Many of the larger signs are treated with the same freedom from pattern, while others, not necessarily more difficult to render, were obviously outlined before painting. Although in some cases, like the △ *di* (*Gr.*[3], X 8, a conical loaf) in the first line, the black outline was no doubt thought to be an appropriate coloration of the sign, it adds nothing and is indeed largely covered in the ⌡ *nsw* (M 23, a reed) at the beginning of the line. The kheker frieze lies within carefully laid out squares and rectangles of red outline.

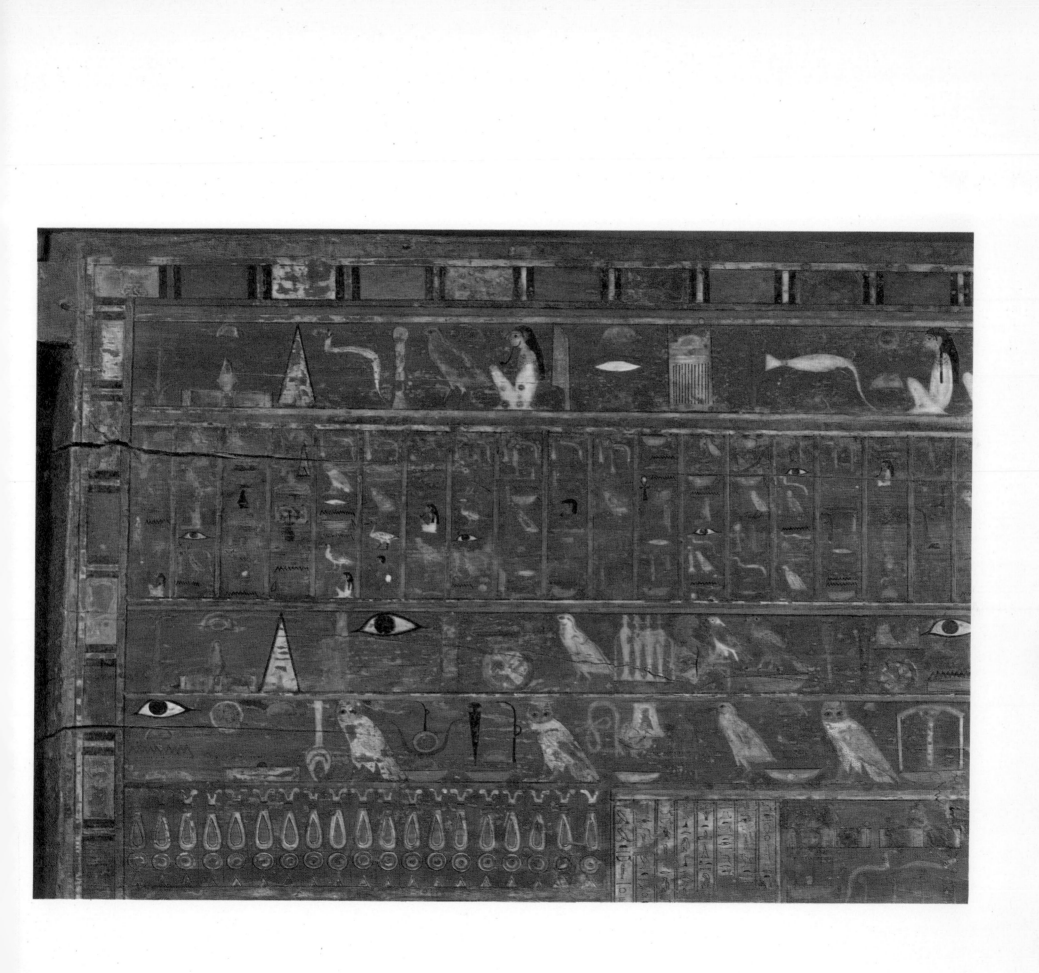

X   THE OFFERING FORMULAE (2)

The slightly different expressions in the faces of the three squatting female determinatives at the left of the first line give good reason for showing caution when trying to interpret facial expression in Egyptian art. In fact, the three are meant to be identical and the slight changes of expression are due to a tilt of a brow or curve of the line of the eye induced through the rapidity with which the subjects were drawn. In the second horizontal line there is a very interesting depiction (in the word *dwȝ* 🖻) of a *d* (*Gr*.[3], D 46, the hand) which once more reveals specifically the hand of the master. Like the right hand of Djehuty-nekht, the line of the finger joints is shown and is curved in such a way as to give the force of perspective. It should also be noted here that the lower edge of the hand is given a more "naturalistic" angle away from the wrist than is usually done in these inscriptions; cf. the much more ideographic rendering just to the right of this example.

The long vertical inscription on the right, which is a speech of a *ẖry-ḥb*-priest (the so-called "lector" priest) about the purification of the offerings presented, the determinative of the word *ẖry-ḥb* 🖼 is a particularly carefully detailed picture of the priest wearing his leopard-skin robe, the ringed tail of which falls between his legs. This charming detail, too, was painted directly without benefit of an outline. Note also the careful treatment of the complex hieroglyph *skr* (the god Sokar) 🖼 : the falcon sits on a gazelle-prowed skiff equipped with two rudder paddles. The skiff in turn rests on a kind of stand which is set on a sledge like the one used to haul the coffin (Fig. 5).

At the far right is the first of a long row (there are two rows actually, separated by vertical inscriptions, see Pls. XIII and XIV) of kneeling offering bearers. He pours some ritual liquid from a *ḥes*-vase (a sacred vessel with lid—of peculiar form shown here—known from earliest times in ancient Egypt), held over his head, into a jar (disintegrated) which he holds with the other hand on the small table in front of him.

XI THE OFFERING FORMULAE AND THE OFFERING BEARERS (1)

The short vertical inscriptions give the names of various offerings, including, among others, oils, beer, wine, onions, etc. Below the lines of inscription is a row of kneeling offering bearers, each of whom is supposed to be carrying the appropriately named item. Thus the seventh bearer from the left holds up a bunch of onions, named in the inscription above slightly to the left. Others are carrying jars and vessels of liquid offerings. The lines of inscription below the offering bearers name further items of the same sort and have their corresponding kneeling bearers (Pls. XIII and XIV). It will be noted that no attempt is made to differentiate between the many kneeling figures except for an occasional change of position in the arms and hands, and that they are given the sketchiest of treatment. Most of the figures were painted without benefit of outline, which relieves them of the completely static quality they would otherwise certainly have.

XII THE OFFERING FORMULAE AND THE OFFERING BEARERS (2)

This plate concludes the list of offerings and has little of special note, except that the forms of the vessels are somewhat more varied than in the preceding plates. The second complete figure from the left is carrying two yellow alabaster jars which are sealed with a skin membrane tied with a string. The lids with black knobs (obsidian ?) are placed on top of the membrane which had been stretched over the open mouths (Jéquier, p. 141).

XIII THE OFFERING BEARERS (1)

The detail shows how rapidly the offering bearers were sketched. The ducks are masterpieces of the painter's technique, and despite the confusion between two overlapping bodies, which is so often a feature of Egyptian art, the vigorous struggles of the living fowl in the firm grasp of their captors is sensitively depicted. Occasionally an effort is made to distinguish individual details in the offering bearers: the third man from the left on the top row has a slightly darker red left arm, to separate it from the body, and the forearm of the first figure in this row is also so distinguished. The several dressed fowl in the middle rows of inscription are neatly trussed with string.

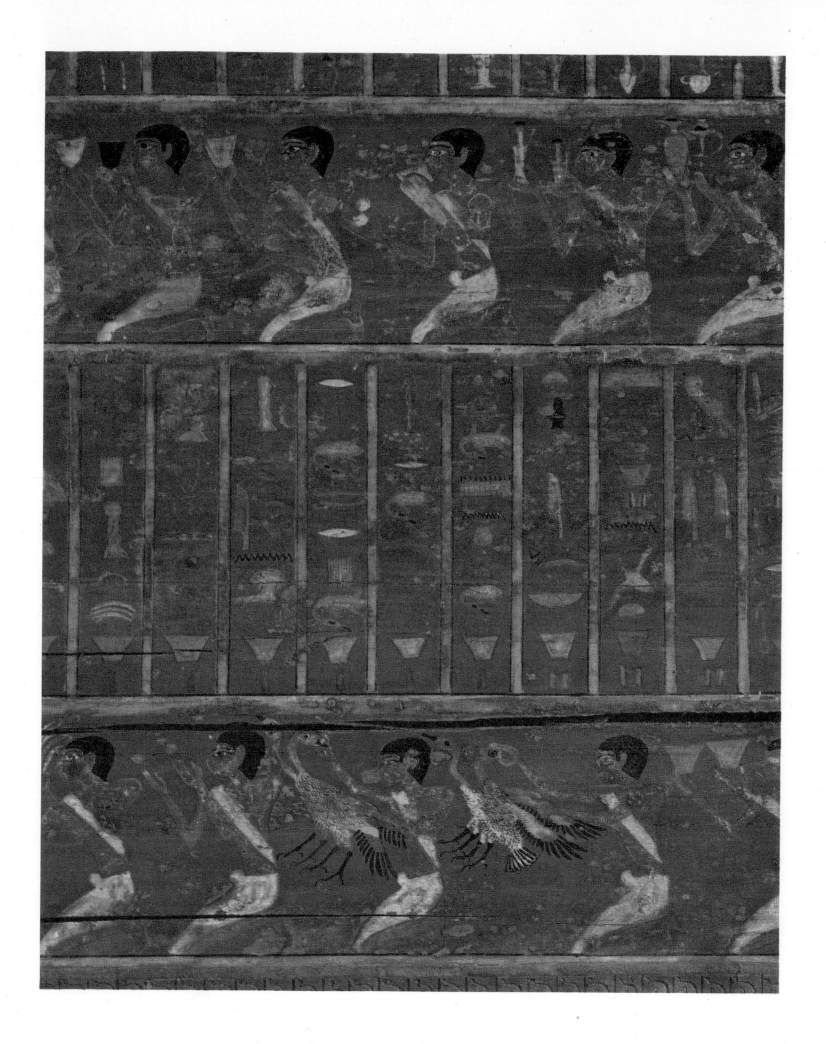

XIV THE OFFERING BEARERS (2)

Several of the figures in this detail were laid out in preliminary outlining before painting, but it in no way detracts from the spontaneity of the final result. The splendid control of the brush is seen in the horns of the oryx head (much of which has disappeared) on the table of offerings in the lower right. The attempt to differentiate between left arm and body is better preserved in this section. The vertical inscriptions come to an end here: the final line states "for the *Ka* of Djehuty-nekht." The determinative after his name is a miniature version of the seated portrait beside the pile of offering (Pl. VIII).

XV THE BED

With this plate we begin the great series of the *Frise des Objets,* the objects of daily life which were thought necessary to the well-being of the *Ka* in the afterlife. The series begins with a bed and some of its accoutrements. The bed, like the chair in Pl. VIII, is developed from the form of a lion, and its feet and legs keep this original form (cf. the bed of Queen Hetep-heres, G. A. Reisner and W. S. Smith, *Giza Necropolis* II [Cambridge, Mass., 1955], pl. 26). What is exceptional here is the extraordinary delicacy and sureness of the drawing and the nice detail of color. The bed itself is made of wood, represented in the curious convention which imitates grain but actually looks much more like the hieroglyphic sign ⌒ (*Gr.*[3] M 3) for a branch of wood. There are several types of headrests, the red one of wood and the white ones of alabaster or a lighter wood.

Above the bed there is a rectangular case which apparently holds four razors (Jéquier, figs. 340–344); the materials of the handles from the top are: ivory (white), grained wood (black and yellow), copper (red), ebony (black). I am not sure what the five dark red objects to the left are: perhaps they are ingots of copper, or are they razors or whetstones (cf. Jéquier, pp. 124 ff)? Below them is some kind of lion-headed board on which are set six rounded pieces of ivory (?); lying directly on the bed is a folded linen cover (Jéquier, fig. 641). The curious object between the collar and copper pieces may be a development of the kilt with frontal strap (the *shendyt*-kilt; cf. Pl. XVIII), a transitional example of which is seen in Jéquier, fig. 60 = fig. 257. Jéquier's example is labeled *ms.t* and appears to be a confusion by the painter of a *shendyt*-kilt (S 26) and the *ms* (F 31), an apron of three foxskins tied together at the top. Jéquier's fig. 255 from another Middle Kingdom coffin is still closer to the object pictured here but, like his fig. 60 (=fig. 257), ends at the bottom with the apron which hangs from the front of the *shendyt*. Jéquier believes that the apron was provided (at least in primitive times) for the protection of the male reproductive organs, and if our curious object is indeed a development from these other representations, it has assumed an entirely stylized amuletic form signifying protection of the sexual organs (cf. *ms* = "to give birth").

The average height of the *Frise* is about .200 m.

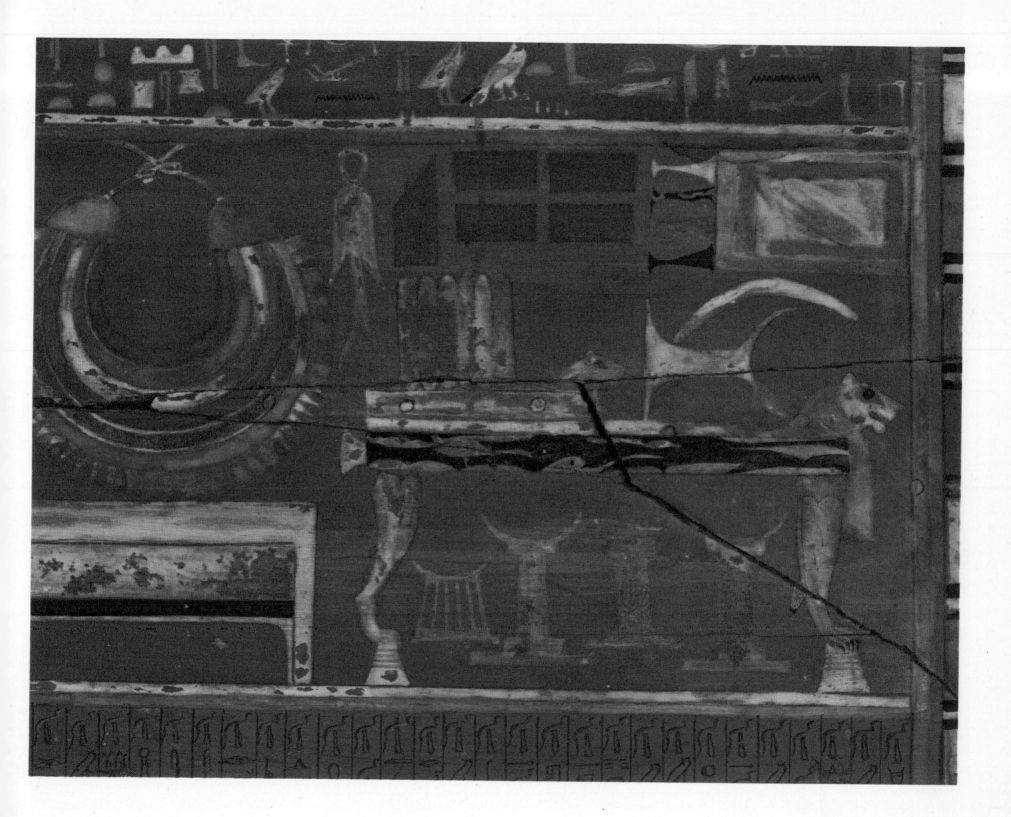

XVI JEWELS AND WEAPONS

Three caskets belong to this row of objects, the end of the middle one being just visible at the far right of this Plate, while the first is found on Pl. XV. The second casket is unfinished but part of it is red. The third is another ivory-and-ebony chest. On this last casket are exposed, as on the others, a collar and counterpoise. This collar has green strands (laid on a red background), probably representing faience despite the inscription above which refers to a collar of lapis lazuli (*ḥsbd*). The counterpoise *mꜥnḫt* is said to consist of precious stones in the label above.

To the left of the jewelry is a group of weapons and staffs. The first of these is the *ḥḳꜣ* ⌐ (*Gr.*[3], S 38) scepter, the symbol of rulership, and here made of gold according to the label. The next item is a forked staff, actual examples of which have been found in Middle Kingdom tombs (Jéquier, pp. 165 ff., especially fig. 431; cf. also H. G. Fischer, "Varia Aegyptiaca," *JARCE* 2 [1963] 23, fig. 1). It is named *ꜥbt*. Two daggers are shown next: one of a yellowish material (gold?) with the tenon for insertion into a handle. The other blade is copper, represented by the dark crimson used so effectively in the modeling of the seated figure of Djehutynekht (Pl. VIII). This time the socket, joining blade and handle, is shown as some black material, and the red outline of the blade's tenon may be seen just above it.

The crooked stick, of yellow wood and tied at the angle, is the hieroglyph *rs* ⌐ (T 13) of unknown purpose (usually associated with bowmen's equipment, Jéquier, p. 223). In the *Frise des Objets* it is usually labeled (as it is here) *pd* *ꜥḥꜥ*. Next comes a white-tipped lance (the tip perhaps made of flint?), followed by eight walking-sticks. The lance and first stick are yellow wood, the others white.

The next item belongs really with the objects in the following plate and will be described there.

XVII   THE FAN AND MIRROR CASE

The central items of this plate are a *tour de force* of drawing and coloration. Surrounding the fan is a crude, very faint, red sketch outline which was not actually followed. In spite of the rough sketch, the master laid out the shape of the fan in white and then, entirely in free-hand, sketched in the spidery greys, blacks and red. The fine detail surely represents prepared papyrus which, stretched on a lightweight ebony framework, would make an admirable fan. Or is it a feather fan? If so, we should expect to see a scale pattern or even proper feathers.

The mirror case, like the decoration surrounding the False Door (Pl. II), is a brilliant piece of basketwork. The minute grey squares were laid down with a rule and then patterned in red, green, blue, and black. The white color had already been put on, filling in the entire shape of the case. The handle of the mirror itself is black ebony. One of the delightful human touches of these paintings, as noted before, is that we can so often see the very hand of the master at work. In this case, we can see from the several overlapping strokes of the brush at the top of the string loop where he made two or three efforts to make his curve a symmetrical one. Indeed we can see where the pigment thinned out in the brush and where he dipped it again into his palette.

Below these two objects are several more caskets of ivory, ebony and red wood, including one seen from its end instead of the side like the others. Two more collars are shown, laid on top of their caskets, and two large red carnelian barrel beads are placed together with four green rectangles which may represent bracelets in another color of faience. At the far right is a beautifully detailed faience beaded girdle of unusual length.

On the left is the first of three sacred mirror standards, the significance of which is quite unclear, made of yellow wood with a green upright edge. The mirror here is silver (although it is labeled gold; in the label the middle one is said to be silver); the third one, seen at the right edge of the next plate, is copper. In the lower left corner of this plate is part of another grained wood chest.

XVIII THE PALETTES AND OTHER ITEMS

The two palettes are as close as we come in these paintings to the craft of the painter himself and, indeed, do not really represent the art itself but rather that of writing. The upper one appears to be made in two pieces, the right end showing the heavy black and yellow grain of the wood, while the other appears to be smoothed off, perhaps from use. A curious feature is that the yellow seems to be laid on the outer edges of this end only, leaving a strip of white down the center in which the two dollops of pigment, red and black, are placed. The second palette is made of white ivory and, like the first, divided into two parts. Perhaps the two black lines represent strings tied around the palette, into which the brushes might be inserted. They might also represent incisions into the palette itself for the insertion of brushes, as found in many actual examples of palettes.

Below the palettes is a table on which are laid a blue-and-white bracelet and an apron-kilt of fine linen. Its color is uncertain: it was either white or yellow and it is impossible to tell from its present state which color it was before oxidation. The edging is blue (changed to green) which is highly unusual. This edging may be dyed blue or blue faience beads which have not been individually detailed. On the other hand, beads of white, green and black are strung along the front of the kilt.

To the left is another wooden chest from which four almost identical bracelets have been taken. The upper two have yellow, probably gold, terminals, while the others have faience terminals. The next group includes an ivory table on which are set four ḥes-vases of blue (turned green), yellow, black and white. The first is labeled lapis lazuli and the second gold. Above these, on the right, are two cowhide cases containing some bladed objects with curving handles. These should be saws (see Pl. XX, upper left), but it would be unusual to find them so elegantly encased. Note that the cowhide covers are similar in convention to black-grained wood. To the right are two yellow vessels of gold and a white ivory tablet (?).

XIX "THE KING'S EQUIPMENT"

       The most prominent items in this section are eight fine white linen sacks, carefully knotted at the top, each containing something carefully labeled "Equipment of the King" without further specification. To the right of these is a group of seven arrows with black feathers and copper and bone or flint tips. The tips are joined to the shafts with copper holders. Perhaps they were disposable tips; after use the shafts could be pulled out of the victims, leaving them ready for insertion of new points.

       The yellow (gold or alabaster) *ḥes*-vase at the far right is set in a tiny canopy imitating the form of a sacred shrine. The next two items are indeterminable. The uprights on the left are green. The covered chest containing four *ḥes*-vases of gold is seen with one side removed, or are we looking at an opened end with the *ḥes*-vases spread out as if seen from the side? Next come four jars, two of them set in vessels with flaring mouths. The yellow jars are gold, the black one perhaps basalt, but the blue (turned green) jar is labeled lapis lazuli, although such a large jar of this material would be a great wonder (like those elsewhere in the frieze) and one requiring a wealth even greater than that apparently held by Djehuty-nekht. Perhaps the two vessels with flaring rims are silver and gold. Above these is an offering table, probably of alabaster, with a loaf, a cake, and a small jar; to the left a red offering table with heads of animals. Once again, in the sheerly drawn horns of the oryx, we see the hand of the master painter, as if we were there. In the upper left corner is a throw-stick or a flail, the handle white and the rest alternating bands of red and white.

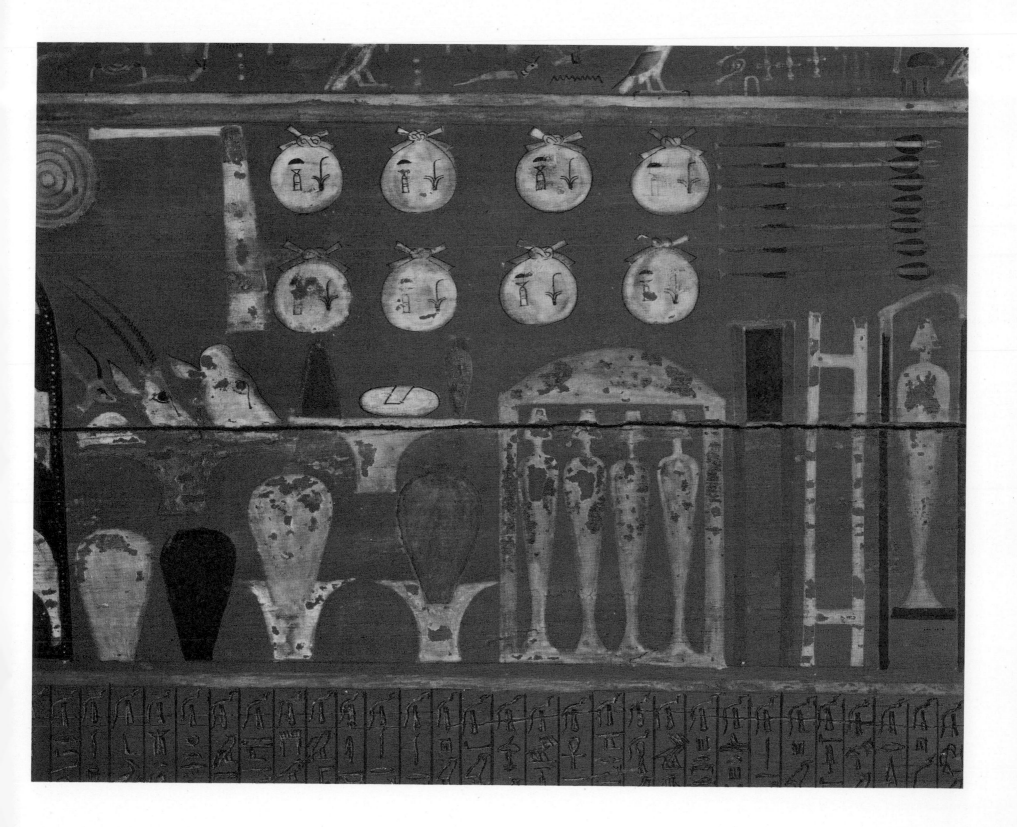

XX TOOLS AND WEAPONS

We have included in the supplementary illustrations (see Fig. 6, p. 15) an excavation photograph of a set of bronze tools with wooden handles found in the Pit 10 B immediately adjacent to Djehuty-nekht's burial place. Comparison of Fig. 6 with the objects shown here demonstrates how faithfully the master of the coffin rendered the actual objects in his own medium. The saw is a duplicate of the one in Fig. 6, except that its blade is longer and the teeth better preserved than those of the original. The two utensils with small splayed ends are chisels. The large bore, having a handle shaped differently from those in Fig. 6, is otherwise like the latter. The drill bow (far left), the axe or hatchet (note the lashings here and in the following), and adze (right) have no simulacra from the nearby burial. The very dark brown red used to represent copper is found occasionally elsewhere. If Djehuty-nekht's tomb had remained to us inviolate, we should probably have found these very items, as well as all the others, or many of them in any case, shown in this great frieze.

Mounted on a red wooden stand is a long cowhide-covered spear-case, from which the sharpened points of the spears protrude. Included in the armory are a cowhide shield (looped at the top for suspension when not in use; note the holes where the cover is sewed onto its frame and the lashings where the handle is tied on the inside) and a cowhide quiver loaded with arrows. I do not know how to explain the disk with yellow and pink concentric circles. I hardly imagine that it is a discus, although it is shown next to the throw-stick (if it be that and not a flail, Pl. XIX). Smith calls my attention to the serpent game in the tomb of Hesy-re, but thinks it improbable here.

The explicit detail of these objects is perhaps the primary reason why we admire them more than any of the hundreds and more of such friezes preserved. It can be seen from Pls. XV–XX how the objects have been organized into compositions of great harmony within themselves. Yet these groups are integrated into the over-all composition seen in Fig. 10.

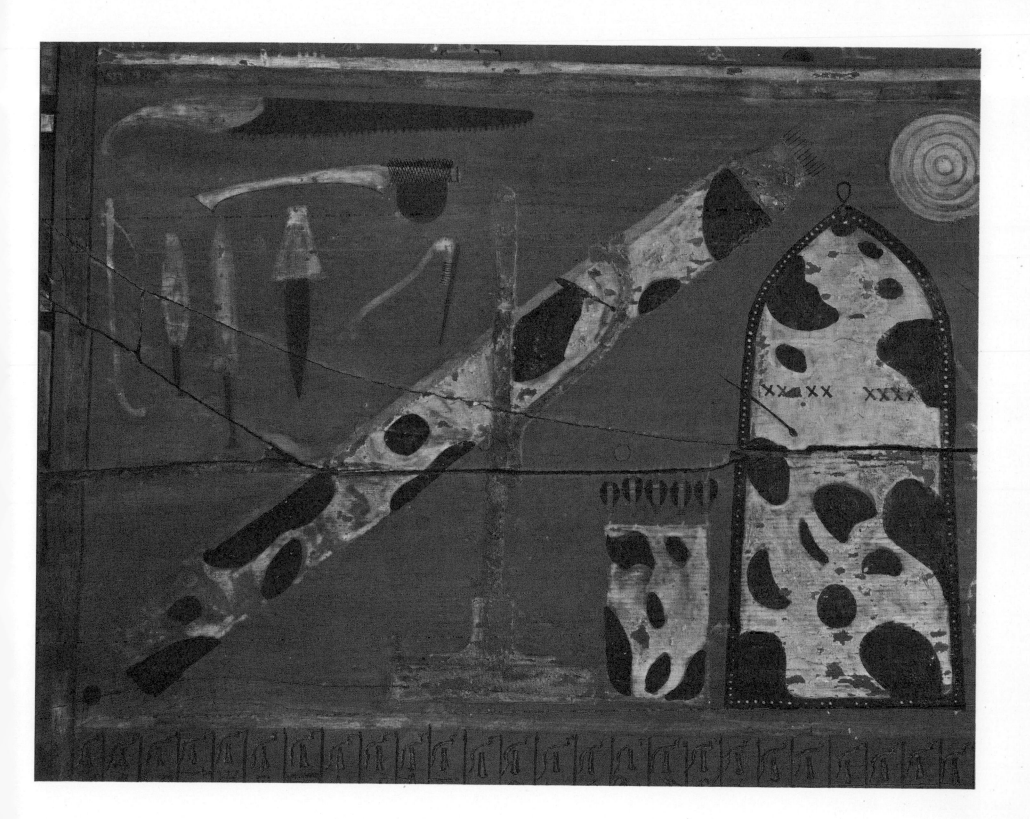

XXI THE LONG FUNERARY INSCRIPTION (1)

The following eleven plates (Pls. XXI–XXXI) are devoted to the long funerary inscription above the *Frise des Objets*. It is an unnecessarily (but typically Egyptian) verbose statement of the good things and state of goodness which will come to Djehuty-nekht as the result of the intercession of the King (unnamed as always) and various deities, ending with that fervent prayer of every ancient Egyptian that the deceased will live, endure, and have dominion forever. The line of smaller inscriptions at the bottom is the long list of labels for the *Frise des Objets*.

As before, our comments are limited to notable features of the drawing and painting. This first plate shows the relationship of the lines of inscription to the *Frise des Objets*. The inscription begins at the upper right.

XXII THE LONG FUNERARY INSCRIPTION (2)

The only details of special note here are the two ducks with different feathering which, in this respect, relates them to the entwined ducks of Pl. VI. It can be noted that both were painted without outline and that grey and black are used with deliberate intent. The four hes-vases 𓎳𓎳 (Gr.[3], W 18, forming the word *hnt*, "in front of," etc.) were carefully centered on vertical lines revealed by the disappearance of their original yellow.

XXIII THE LONG FUNERARY INSCRIPTION (3)

Curiously, in the group of ḥes-vases here there is not a trace of the red outline used in the similar group with such care in the preceding plate. It is also noteworthy that the three god-signs ⌐ (*Gr.*[3], R 8, *nṯr*, apparently a pole with flag) here are quite undecorated, whereas in Pl. X the detail is an interesting feature. On the other hand, care is taken to differentiate two reds in the heart-sign ♡ (F 34, *ib*) on the first line. The method of writing the *n*-sign 〜 (N 35, water), used throughout, is demonstrated clearly in the second and third lines: it was first laid out in black outline and then painted in.

XXIV THE LONG FUNERARY INSCRIPTION (4)

The crested ibis 🦤 (*Gr.*[3], G 25, *ꜣḫ*) in the third line is a pretty piece of drawing with the brush, but unfortunately most of the color is gone. The heart, just to the left in this same line, has an additional band of darker red around its upper edge, a detail which does not appear in the preceding plate. Neither the ▱ (V 30, *nb* wickerwork basket, first line) nor ▱ (V 31, *k*, basket with handle, third line) is given the inner detail they receive in, for instance, Pls. VI and X. On the other hand, the ▫ (Q 3, *p*, stool of reed matting or its cover), below the *k* is partially checkered, but the ⊜ (Aa 1, *ḫ*, placenta?), in the second line, remains unlined. These lapses are curious in view of the labor expended on the coffin, but presumably even a great master is occasionally bored.

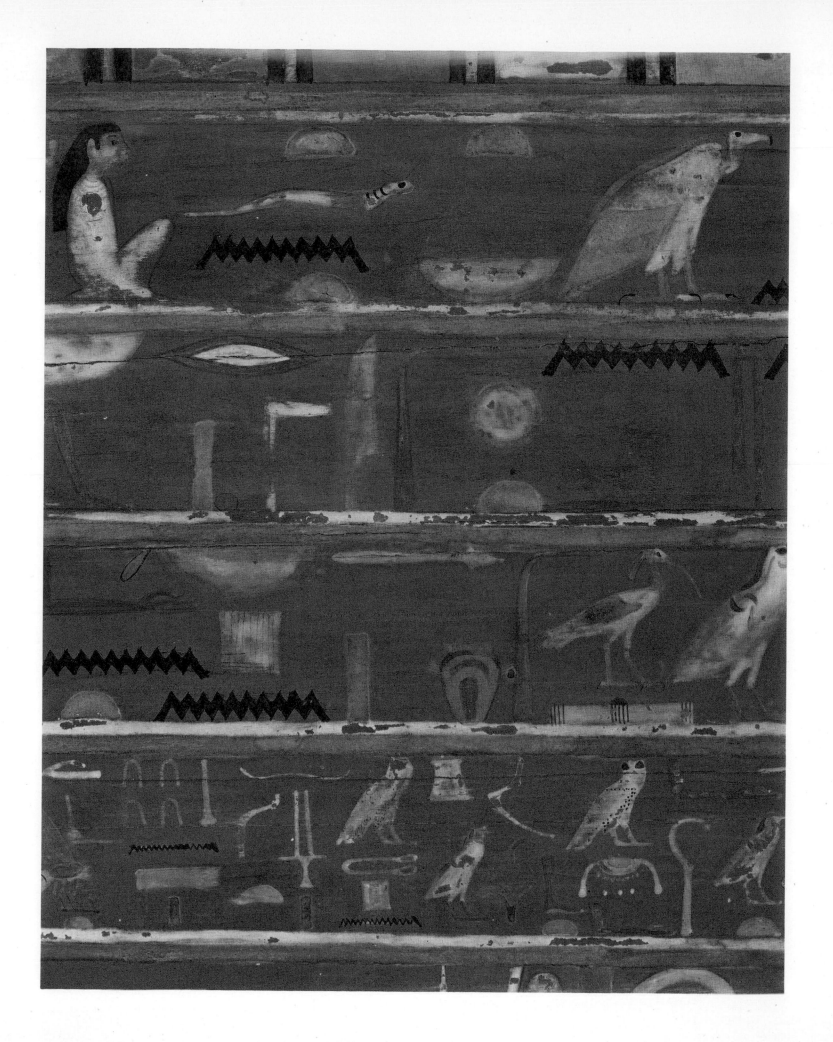

XXV THE LONG FUNERARY INSCRIPTION (5)

There is an inconsistency between the two ducks shown on this plate. Both make up part of the name of the Earth god, Geb, but they appear to be slightly different birds, as shown by the shapes of the bills (that of the lower duck is curved at the end, the other not) and the colors of the legs. Although the feathering is not quite the same in each case, it is close enough not to matter. Whatever the reason for these differences, they are painted with an almost illusionist brush like that which painted the dove (see Pl. VII). The colors are worn off to some extent but the better preserved example on the next plate proves that the smudged wash of grey over the upper feathers of the wings was deliberate. The duck in the first register was outlined in red before painting. It is instructive to compare the use of the black separating the two legs with the inspired painting of the entwined duck in Pl. VI.

The owls (*Gr.*[3], G 17, *m*), which we have seen in several plates, are better preserved here and are comparable in quality to the birds in the ornamental hieroglyphs (Pl. XXXV). Again the outline is used very sparingly; in fact it is not used at all to define the inner edges of the yellow wash of the wings. Finely drawn as they are, the owls are, however, conventional in form.

The speck of red adorning the head of the blue-backed swallow (G 36, *wr*) in the lowest register is a flake detached from the (O 34, *s*, door bolt) just above it and accidentally cemented in its present location.

XXVI THE LONG FUNERARY INSCRIPTION (6)

The duck in the upper left is in a better state of preservation than the several we have just seen and at the same time is more detailed in its treatment. On the back, immediately to the left of the grey wash on the wing, there is a very subtle use of grey strokes which highlight the black and white feathers. The legs were painted in grey before being hatched in black strokes. The red outline which was not precisely followed may be seen easily here.

The quail-chick 𓆑 (*Gr.*[3], G 43, *w*) is a good example of the conventions followed throughout the coffin. Whenever special attention is given to it, feathering is always in grey, black being employed only for the pupil of the eye. Usually, blue feathers are shown on the head and back.

The contrast between "drawing" and "writing" may be seen at once by comparing the carefully drawn hieroglyphs of the large inscription with the hurried writing of the small one.

XXVII THE LONG FUNERARY INSCRIPTION (7)

The figure of a man leaning forward on a staff 𓀉 (*Gr.*³, A 19) is the ideogram for "old age" and in this case refers to Geb, the Earth god, as eldest son of the god Atum. It is a curious convention because it resembles nothing so much as a vigorous young man hurrying forward (although the sign is drawn in a way much more descriptive of old age elsewhere; especially cf. Fischer, *JARCE* 2 [1963] 23, fig. 1). The quail-chicks in this plate were not so detailed as the one in Pl. XXVI and the only feathery strokes are red along the rump. The eyes, too, are red spots only.

That the color conventions could alternate with ease may be seen in the blue *ankh*-signs ☥ (S 34, the ties of a sandal) in the large inscription. In Pl. XXVI, in the small inscription, they are black with white filling. For the interchange of conventional colors in the Old Kingdom, including blue for black, see *OKSP*², pp. 257–263.

XXVIII THE LONG FUNERARY INSCRIPTION (8)

The ⸚ (*Gr.*³, I 10, *d*, cobra) usually has a white belly and yellow back and the neck is invariably blue. In the best examples, the back is spotted and the treadlike belly lined; sometimes these details are red, as in the center of the second line here, and sometimes black (Pl. XXIX, first line). Only the back of the serpent shown here is preserved, leaving the belly strokes exposed like a hairy growth. The horned viper ⸚ (I 9, *f*) usually has the same coloration, although the body-marking is indicated by cross-hatching. The painter began to stroke over in black the red leaf markings in the reed-leaf ⸚ (M 17, *i*) on the third line, but apparently tired of it.

XXIX THE LONG FUNERARY INSCRIPTION (9)

When coming to paint the duck in the first line, the master found the preliminary red sketch quite unsatisfactory and ignored much of it. Although this section seems to have suffered more than most from deterioration, there is no trace of red on the branch of wood ⤳ (Gr.[3], M 3, nḫt). If anything, it was painted yellow, whereas the convention followed throughout elsewhere is red. Smith has called my attention to the fact that the fingers and thumb holding the cone of bread in the sign rdi ⌂ (D 37) on the second line are shown in proper form, with the thumb going behind the cone to grasp its other side.

XXX THE LONG FUNERARY INSCRIPTION (10)

The two plates concluding the long funerary inscription are too poorly preserved to call for much comment. We may only point out that in the third line Djehuty-nekht's name is abbreviated to Djehuty, followed by the determinative of the seated man holding a staff in the left hand and some other object in the right (a short rod or piece of linen?—see B. von Bothmer, *BMFA* 48 [1950], 10 ff.). The bent arm holding a flail ᴧ▱ (*Gr.*³, D 43, *ḏsr*), just following the seated man, is important for trying to determine the nature of the objects shown in Pls. XVI, XIX. In the hieroglyph the flail ends in the long pendants which one expects, whereas in the *Frise des Objets,* it will be recalled, all the bands are horizontal.

XXXI THE LONG FUNERARY INSCRIPTION (11)

Here we need note only the prominent use of two of the reds which are a feature of these paintings. The dark brown-red was used here for the sign ⵣ (*Gr.*[3], U 15, *tm* = *itm*, Atum's name written, apparently, as a kind of sledge), whereas blue was used for the same sign in Pl. XXVII. This is the same dark red used to signify copper or bronze in the tools below (the blade of the saw is seen at the bottom of the plate). Elsewhere the usual bright, rather orange red is used.

XXXII THE ORNAMENTAL HIEROGLYPHS (1)

The following twelve plates (Pls. XXXII–XLIII) are devoted to the two lines of painted inscription on the lid of the coffin. To call these inscriptions "ornamental" is to deny their highly important, indeed basic, function: the vital recitation of the spells for the future welfare of Djehuty-nekht. In three ways these painted inscriptions meet what, for want of a better term, we might call the standard of Middle Kingdom painting: the purity of the color, the perfection of form, the spaciousness of the composition.

In the Great Offering Scene, the master of the Bersheh Coffin was the great innovator; here he is the master of tradition. In some ways, these inscriptions reveal him to be more the painter than the draftsman. Although the forms are as graceful and elegant as ever, the preliminary outline is almost nonexistent here and the forms are created directly with the brush instead of the pen, as it were.

The *nsw* (*Gr.*³, M 23) is painted with green pigment so thick that we can still see the strokes of the brush as it was swept out in painting the leaves. The *b*₃-bird (G 29) is a good example of what I mean by painting as opposed to drawing. Here was a good chance to play with feathering and to create the same effects found on the ducks in the other inscriptions. Instead, only a few strokes are used, and the effect relies wholly on the contrast of the white and blue pigments. The feet were yellow with black nails. The '₃-column (O 29) was originally yellow, now faded to white, reflecting its origin as a wooden column. Even it, difficult enough to draw, was painted directly without outline. The *ankh*-sign has the little tufts at the end of its arms, signifying its original form as a sandal strap.

The pleasing visual effect of the incised Coffin Texts below must be ascribed entirely to the inherently decorative quality of hieroglyphic signs as a means of writing. In fact, these are not especially well cut but the moving line of their forms causes the eye to see them as a surface of rippling movement. They were first written out in black, then incised.

The height of each register of painted inscriptions is about .105 m.

XXXIII THE ORNAMENTAL HIEROGLYPHS (2)

Here the owl is a marvel of drawing, while the vulture *mwt* (*Gr.*[3], G 14) is pure painting. In neither case, however, was an outline drawn first. The *ḥt*-sign (F 32), thought to be the belly of an animal with its tail, is black and white, the black spines representing teats.

XXXIV THE ORNAMENTAL HIEROGLYPHS (3)

The two squatting women, completely wrapped in white linen, are the determinatives of feminine names and words. They are made especially charming here because the painter has gone to the trouble of manipulating his brush around the lips and chins, a detail which does not occur in the rows of male offering bearers (Pls. XIII–XIV). In this plate, an outline occurs at last, but only around the s ‖ ($Gr.^3$, S 29, bolt of folded cloth). The downturned arms ⌒ (D 35, n, signifying negation) wear white bracelets.

XXXV   THE ORNAMENTAL HIEROGLYPHS (4)

Unfortunately, the hare has suffered to some extent since the coffin was excavated (this is one of the rare cases where significant post-excavation damage may be observed). Enough remains to show that the master lingered here and put all his inspiration into the subject. The body was painted white and over this ochre and yellow were washed, leaving the white exposed here and there. Then black and grey were added. A few wisps of grey around the haunch reveal another glimpse of three-dimensional form, so subtle that it might not have been intended. The fine whiskers on the nose are almost invisible. The ears are inspired: they could so easily have been made static by heavy outlining, but instead the outlines are broken, incomplete, and give that same uncertainty of spatial consciousness that is the genius of the master of the coffin.

Once more the owls stand out in their perfection of form and detail. From our point of view, the reds of the heart signs could not be better placed in this composition of tawny colors.

The wing of a door ⟳ (*Gr.*[3], O 31), the determinative of the word *wn* 🐇 made up with the hare and *n* and meaning "to open," is an especially interesting and factual portrayal of the actual object. It is made of four horizontal slabs of white wood and its pointed post for turning in a socket is apparently fitted with a metal tip. The other end of the post is squared.

Altogether, this group of signs may be taken as one of the high points of the coffin.

XXXVI THE ORNAMENTAL HIEROGLYPHS (5)

The stains and damage are from water-spotting in the 1920 shipboard fire. The primary damage is a slight fading of the colors, which were certainly as fresh as those of their neighbors when excavated (cf. Fig. 11). The now very pale vase was once a fine yellow alabaster. Despite the water damage the pure, powdery blue, seen so fleetingly in tiny details elsewhere, shows well here. The exceptional use of the outline may be noted again and, as frequently before, appears only when the objects depicted are red.

XXXVII THE ORNAMENTAL HIEROGLYPHS (6)

Here the colors of the ornamental hieroglyphs are preserved with a clarity and purity which must come very close to their appearance when they were freshly painted. As in the preceding plate, the blue (except on and under the serpent) comes through in the astonishing pure tone that seems to be apprehended by more senses than merely the visual one. Had this blue survived in the many other parts of the coffin where it is used, these paintings would probably have an even greater impact than the one—already so intense—they now have. This section forms a kind of microcosm of what we admire so much in Middle Kingdom painting: the superb drawing, the softness and clarity of the coloration, the clean spatial organization.

Three reds are used here. In the downturned arms, as in the inner details of $\downarrow$ ($Gr.^3$, F 35, *nfr,* heart and windpipe), two are used together. The arms are colored in the intermediate red, but the left wrist and hand is a darker red. On the right the transition between the two is difficult to perceive because it has become confused with the outline which is the same color. The ventricles of the heart were first painted the light red used for body color as in the case of the kneeling man, and over these were put patches of dark red. The stem of the windpipe was painted yellow and the heart a very pale ochre. A highly unusual feature is the separation of the fingers in white. In fact the entire hieroglyph seems to have been painted in white, the red laid on afterward and in so doing, leaving exposed the "empty" space between the fingers. It is also notable that this sign is asymmetrical, to take into account empty areas of different sizes on either side of the small owl. The man who bends over tries to stop a flow of black blood. The figure is the determinative of the verb $m(w)$ *t,* "to die" (cf. A 14).

XXXVIII THE ORNAMENTAL HIEROGLYPHS (7)

The face of the squatting lady is pale yellow. Although expected in the same determinatives in Pl. XXXIV, no trace is discernible. It is a great pity that the blues of the vulture have not survived in their original state; the glowing color still seen in Pl. XXXVII would have had a remarkable impact as it was used here with white highlights around each feather. Although in other inscriptions of much lesser quality the *ḥtp*-sign ⌐ (*Gr.*[3], R 4) frequently has details of the loaf ⊖ (X 2) and the reed mat on which it rests, throughout this coffin the sign is painted in the most conventional way, usually green.

XXXIX THE ORNAMENTAL HIEROGLYPHS (8)

The serpent this time has a red head. The now dark blue-green coloring (not discernible here) of the quail-chick 𓆎 (*Gr.*³, G 43) has an added intensity, due to the use of black outline to separate the originally blue areas from the yellow (now faded almost to white, as frequently throughout). The twisted rope *ḥ* 𓎛 (V 28) is well preserved here. Although they are frequently green, the *t*-signs ⌒ (X 1) in this section are blue, now oxidized.

XL THE ORNAMENTAL HIEROGLYPHS (9)

The formerly blue back of the swallow 𓅨 (*Gr.*[3], G 36, *wr*) has black markings; some strokes of the original blue are still preserved in the white tail. The markings of the falcon *ḥr* 𓅃 (G 5) are black.

XLI THE ORNAMENTAL HIEROGLYPHS (10)

By the time he reached this part of the inscription, the painter discovered that space was running out and he had to crowd the signs. The result is the relatively careless disposition of the signs on this and the succeeding plates. Nor are the colors in as good a state of preservation as the preceding, although the water spot does not reach the area. Fortunately there are no new signs of significance. The only new detail of any interest is *imy* ╫ (*Gr.*[3], Z 11), which is shown here as a black bar crossing a white one. The proportions are somewhat unusual: generally the vertical bar is much longer than the other.

XLII THE ORNAMENTAL HIEROGLYPHS (11)

There is one especially unusual sign here: , which is an archaic form of *Gr.*³, M 36, a bunch of flax tied together (cf. Hilda Petrie, *Egyptian Hieroglyphs of the First and Second Dynasties,* pl. xx, nos. 473 ff. Also cf. *Gr.*³, M 37–38 with references). The flax is yellow with red markings. Note that the *nb*-baskets are shown to have woven patterns. The ⌐ arm (D 41) has white spaces between the fingers, as in Pl. XXXVII.

XLIII THE ORNAMENTAL HIEROGLYPHS (12)

The inscription concludes saying "The Osiris, this Djehuty-nekht, forever!" The colors are but a poor reflection of their former beauty, but the forms shine through clear and graceful as before. One of the essential qualities of the Egyptian concept of form is its precision of definition, a definition created by an immaculate outline which produces form. The form is thus freed of all extraneous relationships, even space. We might go so far as to say that the innovations of the Great Offering Scene make it imperfect from the Egyptian point of view, and if these innovations had been lost by the removal of the color, the significance which we have imparted to them would have been as nothing. Here, where much of the color is gone, not so much of the aesthetic expression is lost because it was, after all, the line-created form that was supremely important. In this sense we may perhaps ascribe to the color of these paintings the significance of an attribute rather than a quality.

XLIV THE STONE VESSELS

If we did not know from his sculptures in stones of many kinds that the ancient Egyptian had a profound feeling for the qualities of the various materials, we would know it from his paintings of them. Such is the case of the granite or breccia jar shown in this plate. It is probably granite because the conventions are those usually used to represent it, but it is in fact more specifically like breccia which has sharp, angular crystals in the black stone. The jar was first laid out in white and then covered over with short strokes of the heaviest black, some straight, others curving, but the whole executed at random and without the highly refined order found in every other painting on the coffin. The lid is made of some other material, perhaps wood or pottery, and has the appearance of a material turned on wheel or lathe. The knob handle is perhaps obsidian. Jars such as this, with lug-handles, are known especially from the Old Kingdom.

The tall jar immediately to the left was once a lovely piece of banded alabaster, but the pinkish bands are now almost lost. Note that the jar is sealed with red membrane. The other two jars are of similar materials, only the red tops are lighter and the jar at the far left is banded alabaster.

On the right are two linen bags containing green and black eye-paint, staples of the Egyptian toilet since Predynastic times. They might so easily have been disks outlined by the bags, but the master has given them the amorphous shapes of their natural condition. At the far right are two unstrung bows. The objects sit on wooden tables, although the possibility exists that these are really chests.

This vignette is taken from the head-end of the coffin on which a total of eighteen oils and materials of various kinds are listed for the well-being of the deceased. Shown here are the vessels containing them. The remainder of the series is too poorly preserved to illustrate.

The height of the register of vessels is about .140 m.

XLV THE PROCESSION OF OFFERING BEARERS

Although the complete series of models of daily life from the tomb of Djehuty-nekht will be published in a subsequent volume, mention must be made of this unparalleled piece of wooden sculpture. The procession of three lithesome girls is led by what we suppose to be a priest who carries over his shoulder a large *hes*-vase painted dark brown-red to represent copper and in his right hand a mirror in a gaily colored cowhide case (cf. the mirror case in Pl. XVII). The case was made of tanned leather with a patch of cowhide sewed onto it. The grey-green strips around the cowhide show black stitching. These strips are one more example of the remarkable refinement of the painter. A light green was first painted over the white undercoating and on this was brushed a green with a touch of black in it. The case is a single piece of wood hollowed out very finely to fit over the black (representing ebony) handled mirror (not actually made; a tenon is attached to the handle). The vase was originally pegged to the priest's hand. His face, carved in a separate piece, is held to the back of the head by a tiny peg set through the filtrum.

The middle lady carries a basket of clay-stoppered jars (apparently the stoppers are scored, if this be what the black mud strips on white represent), and the lady in front of her a covered basket. Whatever the lady in the rear carried, it was apparently held with both hands. Clutched in her right fist is a bit of peg. In her left palm is a peg hole and another is found just above this hand in the side of the wig. The ducks which the first two ladies carry have separately made necks and wings, while the delicately carved legs are cut in the same piece as the bodies.

The arms of the figures are made separately and fitted to the bodies with tiny pegs. The bent left arms of the first three figures are made in two pieces carefully fitted together in open half-lap joints with dowel locks. Although the girls are barefoot, the priest wears sandals, the straps of which are painted in white. A full discussion of this sculpture is given by the writer in "The Entourage of an Egyptian Governor," *BMFA* 66 (1968), 5–27.

The figures are unusually graceful and are masterpieces of Middle Kingdom sculpture. The modeling is very naturalistic, especially in the treatment of the hip and thigh structure, around the breasts and in the abdomens. The dresses cling to the flesh like skin. The tall, elongated proportions are typical of the later Twelfth Dynasty and may be seen in the nearly contemporary ladies of Djehuty-hetep's court (see Chapter V). The workmanship is so fine that we might expect it to come from the master of the coffin, but this is unlikely, since the two crafts were almost always separated. However, it is certain that the master painted the wooden figures

because the palette and its delicate use are the same as that found on the coffin. Furthermore, the details of the baskets are exactly like those of the painted baskets, Pls. IV and VI.

Anyone who today has seen the country women of Egypt as they carry their bundles proudly and gracefully on their heads will not wonder at the elegance which distinguishes these remarkable figures.

XLVI OFFERINGS CARRIED TO A MAN NAMED TWAU
Wall Painting from Tomb 359, Naga ed-Deir

This plate illustrates how the traditional Memphite style survived to a certain extent during the First Intermediate Period in Upper Egypt. The painting was copied by Norman de Garis Davies when he was working for Reisner at Naga ed-Deir at the beginning of this century. The classical unities continue in the well-drawn figures of the offering bearers, and the procession has the sense of regulated determination known during the Old Kingdom. But a new color sense has entered the scene, especially in the pinkish-orange, blue and yellow ducks. The colors are used for their own sake as a decorative pattern. The pointing with black dots is another new development. The representation of whiskered men was not unknown before, but here it receives an interesting treatment in the first man on the right, on whose cheeks and chin a stubbly black beard is drawn. Despite the relatively well-formed proportions of the men, the fowl are out of scale. In this respect, the painting comes closer to developments typical of the Intermediate Period.

XLVII A MARSH SCENE IN THE TOMB
OF UKH-HETEP
Wall Painting from Tomb C 1, Ukh-hetep III, Meir

One of the most remarkable monuments of the Middle Kingdom is the tomb of Ukh-hetep III at Meir in Middle Egypt. All the decoration is executed in paint (except for some details of kilts modeled in plaster), and the colors used are amongst the purest and clearest known from ancient Egypt. In this detail from a swamp scene, a song bird has alighted on the branch of a marsh plant, the leaves of which change color as if wafted by a breeze. On another branch a frog appears ready to leap into the water. At the top is the bottom of a papyrus skiff from which Ukh-hetep is hunting fowl.

The transparent colors of this detail are found throughout Ukh-hetep's paintings and are typical of the colors used at Meir throughout the Twelfth Dynasty.

XLVIII   UKH-HETEP'S GREEN-STRIPED CLOAK
Wall Painting from Tomb C 1, Ukh-hetep III, Meir

Much of the painting in Ukh-hetep's tomb uses the technique of stippling which can only be a conscious effort to bring light into the colors. The effect of this usage is most astonishing in the treatment of a cloak worn by the Nomarch, a detail of which is shown here. The horizontal pleats were first outlined in light red. Immediately below this line was drawn a thin green line. Next comes heavy stippling in green, which decreases in intensity until the white background is left clean. The two lowermost outlines are grey because the green outlines cover the red lines. The grey dress over which the striped cloak was thrown is nearly transparent. The legs are dark brown-red under this dress. The uncovered parts of the legs were first painted light red. On this color is a darker red stippling. This is one of the most remarkable paintings in Egypt before the Eighteenth Dynasty.

In a small fragment of painted relief from the Deir el Bahari temple of Neb-hepet-re Mentuhotep now in the Boston Museum (07.537), a somewhat similar idea was used. Only a bit of the white kilt of a striding man is shown. On it are painted light red horizontal stripes. The upper part of these stripes is painted over with a strip of darker red, giving a suggestion of the shading which is so successfully rendered on Ukh-hetep's cloak.

XLIX GATHERING GRAIN
Wall Painting from Tomb 2, Djehuty-hetep, Bersheh

Djehuty-hetep's tomb at Bersheh does not experiment with the effects of light and color in the way the masters of Djehuty-nekht and Ukh-hetep did. However, his painter was moved to use the clear tones of color which were noted especially at Meir and which are also found on the coffin which is the subject of this book. Moreover, Djehuty-hetep's painter had as light and delicate a brush as that used in the other monuments. The refinement of the drawing is observed here especially in the treatment of the sheaves of grain and in the feathery ruff along the back of the donkey's neck. Stippling of the muzzle reminds one of the interest in breaking up the surface seen at Naga ed-Deir (Pl. XLVI) and particularly at Meir (Pl. XLVIII). See *AJA* 55(1951) 323, fig. 1, for a suggested location of this fragment.

L DAILY LIFE FROM THE TOMB
OF DJEHUTY-HETEP
Wall Painting from Tomb 2, Djehuty-hetep, Bersheh

In the upper register women are winnowing grain, shown as small grains flying in the air against a ground plan of the area in which the activity takes place. Below two men appear to be putting something into a row of vessels (see *AJA* 55[1951] 323, fig. 1, for the lower part of the fragment). The hieroglyph between them is the drill *wbꜣ* ⌇ (*Gr.*³, U 27), meaning "to bore" and "to open," but its use here is uncertain.

The refined drawing of the profiles and crinkly hair is executed with the greatest facility. It is to be noted that an outline does not occur on the surface, although original drawing lines may lie under the paint.

LI   A VINE
Wall Painting from Tomb 2, Djehuty-hetep, Bersheh

Most of the small fragments rearranged here are the only remnants of a vine which grows on red stalks or supporting poles. The fragment on the right comes from the grape arbor in another section of this wall. See *AJA* 55(1951) 325, fig. 2. Curiously, the vine grows against a red-spotted pink (more ochre in the largest fragment) background, which is the usual convention for showing the pebbly desert. In the midst of the vine is the corner of a green basket. The yellow flowers are not unlike the white blossoms found in the marsh in Pl. XLVII. The twisting tendril of the grape vine, the curving branches of the other vine and its delicately formed leaves and flowers relate the painting to the branch in Pl. V and to the painting of Wah-ka II at Qau el Kebir (*Antaeopolis,* pl. XXV).

ILLUSTRATIONS OF THE COFFIN

7. *Above,* Exterior of outer coffin: left side (B 2519)
8. *Below,* Exterior of outer coffin: right side (B 2521)

9. *Top,* Interior of outer coffin: left side (A 2213)
10. *Above,* Interior of outer coffin: right side (A 2214)
11. *Below,* Interior of outer coffin: lid (A 2220)

12. *Above,* Interior of outer coffin: head end

13. *Below,* Map of "The Two Ways" on the right side of Djehuty-nekht's inner coffin (A 2899 and 2900)

CHRONOLOGY

The chronology used here follows exactly the one used by the editors of *CAH²*, as published in the fascicles *CAH²*, vol. I, ch. XIV, and *CAH²*, vol. I, ch. XX.

Old Kingdom

Fourth Dynasty	*ca.* 2613–2494
Fifth Dynasty	*ca.* 2494–2345
Sixth Dynasty	*ca.* 2345–2181

First Intermediate Period

Seventh Dynasty	*ca.* 2181–2173
Eighth Dynasty	*ca.* 2173–2160
Ninth Dynasty	*ca.* 2160–2130
Tenth Dynasty	*ca.* 2130–2040

Middle Kingdom

Eleventh Dynasty	2133–1991
Mentuhotep I ⎫ Intef I ⎭	2133–2118
Intef II	2117–2069
Intef III	2068–2061
Neb-hepet-re Mentuhotep II	2060–2010
Sankh-ka-re Mentuhotep III	2009–1998
Neb-tawy-re Mentuhotep IV ⎫ The god's Father Sesostris ⎭	1997–1991
Twelfth Dynasty	1991–1786
Amenemhat I	1991–1962
Sesostris I	1971–1928
Amenemhat II	1929–1895
Sesostris II	1897–1878
Sesostris III	1878–1843
Amenemhat III	1842–1797
Amenemhat IV	1798–1790
Sebekneferu	1789–1786

BIBLIOGRAPHY AND ABBREVIATIONS

AAAE: W. S. Smith, *Art and Architecture of Ancient Egypt* (Baltimore, reprinted with corrections 1965)

Acc. No.: Accession Number

Ancient Egypt[4]: W. S. Smith, *Ancient Egypt as represented in the Museum of Fine Arts, Boston* (Boston, fourth edition, 1960)

Ancient Egyptian Paintings: Nina M. Davies and Alan H. Gardiner, *Ancient Egyptian Paintings* (Chicago, 1936)

Antaeopolis: W. M. F. Petrie, *Antaeopolis: the Tombs of Qau* (London, 1930)

Anthes, *Hatnub:* R. Anthes, *Die Felseninschriften von Hatnub* (Leipzig, 1928)

ASAE: Annales du Service des Antiquités de l'Égypte

Badawy, A., *A History of Egyptian Architecture, the First Intermediate Period, the Middle Kingdom, and the Second Intermediate Period* (Berkeley and Los Angeles, 1966)

Barta, *Opferliste:* W. Barta, *Die altägyptische Opferliste von der Frühzeit zur griechisch-römischen Epoche* (Berlin, 1963)

Beni Hasan: P. E. Newberry, *Beni Hasan* I–IV (London, 1893–1900)

El Bersheh: P. E. Newberry and F. Ll. Griffith, *El Bersheh,* vols. I–II (London, [1896])

BIFAO: Bulletin de l'Institut français d'Archéologie orientale du Caire

BMFA: Bulletin of the Museum of Fine Arts, Boston

BMMA: Bulletin of the Metropolitan Museum of Art, New York

de Buck, A., *The Egyptian Coffin Texts,* vols. I–VIII (Chicago, 1935–1947: OIP 34, 49, 64, 67, 73, 81, 87)

CAH[2]: *Cambridge Ancient History,* revised edition issued in fascicles

Cairo *Guide:* United Arab Republic, Ministry of Tourism and Antiquities, Antiquities Department, The Egyptian Museum, Cairo, *A Brief Description of the Principal Monuments* (Cairo, 1966)

Černý, J., *Ancient Egyptian Religion* (London, 1952)

CG: Cairo, *Catalogue générale du Musée égyptien*

Chassinat, E., and Palanque, Ch., *Une campagne de fouilles dans la nécropole d'Assiout = MIFAO* 24 (1911)

Davies, Nina de G., and Gardiner, A. H., *Tomb of Amenemhet* (London, 1915)

Davies, Norman de G., *Five Theban Tombs* (London, 1913)

Davies, Norman de G., *The Tomb of Antefoker* (London, 1920)

Deir el Gebrawi: Norman de G. Davies, *The Rock Tombs of Deir el Gebrawi,* vols. I–II (London, 1902)

Dunham, Dows, "The Tomb of Dehuti-Nekht and His Wife," *BMFA* 19 (1921), 43 ff.

Dunham, Dows, *The Egyptian Department and Its Excavations* (Boston, 1958)

Exp. No.: Expedition Number

Farina, Giulio, *La Pittura Egiziana* (Milan, 1929)

Faulkner, *Concise Dictionary:* R. O. Faulkner, *A Concise Dictionary of Middle Egyptian* (Oxford, 1962)

Firth, C. M., and Gunn, B., *Teti Pyramid Cemeteries* (Cairo, 1926)

Frankfort, H., *Ancient Egyptian Religion* (New York, 1948)

Frankfort, H., *Kingship and the Gods* (Chicago, 1948)

Gardiner, A. H., *Egypt of the Pharaohs* (Oxford, 1961)

Gauthier, H., *Dictionnaire des noms géographiques contenus dans les textes hiéroglyphiques* (Paris, 1925–1929)

Gr.[3]: A. H. Gardiner, *Egyptian Grammar* (Oxford, third edition, 1957); the letter and number which follow *Gr.*[3] in our references pertain to the hieroglyph which may be found in Gardiner's index of signs, pp. 544–547.

Groenewegen-Frankfort, H., *Arrest and Movement* (London, 1951)

Hayes, W. C., *The Scepter of Egypt,* vol. I. (New York, 1953)

Helck, *Beamtentiteln:* H. W. Helck, *Untersuchungen zu den Beamtentiteln des ägyptischen alten Reiches* (Glückstadt, 1954)

JARCE: Journal of the American Research Center in Egypt

JE: Cairo, *Journal d'éntree du Musée égyptien*

JEA: Journal of Egyptian Archaeology

Jéquier: G. Jéquier, *Les frises des objets des sarcophages du moyen empire = MIFAO* 47 (1921)

Jéquier, G., *Le monument funéraire du Pepi II,* vols. I–II (Cairo, 1936–1940)

Klebs, L., *Die Reliefs und Malereien des Mittleren Reiches* (Heidelberg, 1922)

Lacau, *Sarcophages:* P. Lacau, *Sarcophages antérieurs au nouvel empire,* vols. I–II (Cairo, 1904–1906)

Lucas[4]: A. Lucas, revised by J. R. Harris, *Ancient Egyptian Materials and Industries* (London, fourth edition, 1962)

Manuel: J. Vandier, *Manuel d'Archéologie égyptienne,* vols. I–IV (Paris, 1952–1964)

MDAIK: Mitteilungen des Deutschen Archäologischen Instituts Abteilung Kairo

Meir: A. M. Blackman, *The Rock Tombs of Meir,* vols. I–VI (London, 1914–1953)

Meket-rēʿ: H. E. Winlock, *Models of Daily Life in Ancient Egypt from the Tomb of Meket-rēʿ at Thebes* (Cambridge, Mass., 1955)

MFA: Museum of Fine Arts, Boston

"A Middle Kingdom Painted Coffin": Dows Dunham and W. S. Smith, "A Middle Kingdom Painted Coffin from Deir El Bersheh," *Scritti in Onore di Ippolito Rosellini,* vol. I. (Pisa, 1949) 263 ff. and pls. XXI–XXVII

MIFAO: Mémoires publiés par les membres de l'Institut français d'Archéologie orientale du Caire

MMA: Metropolitan Museum of Art, New York

Moʿalla: J. Vandier, *Moʿalla, la tombe d'Anthtifi et la tombe de Sébekhotep* (Cairo, 1950)

Montet, P., *Géographie de l'Égypte ancienne,* vols. I–II (Paris, 1958–1961)

Müller, H. W., *Alt-ägyptische Malerei* (Berlin, 1959)

Müller, H. W., "Egyptian Art" article in *Encyclopedia of World Art,* vol. IV (New York, 1961)

Müller, H. W., *Die Felsengräber der Fürsten von Elephantine* (Glückstadt, 1940)

Naville, E., *The XIth Dynasty Temple at Deir el-Bahari,* vols. I–III (London, 1907–1913)

Neg. No.: Negative Number

OIP: Oriental Institute Publication

OKSP[2]: W. S. Smith, *A History of Egyptian Sculpture and Painting in the Old Kingdom* (Cambridge, Mass., second edition, 1949)

"A Painting . . . of Hepzefa": W. S. Smith, "A Painting in the Assiut Tomb of Hepzefa," *MDAIK* 15 (1957), 221 ff.

"Paintings . . . at Bersheh": W. S. Smith, "Paintings of the Egyptian Middle Kingdom at Bersheh," *AJA* 55 (1951), 321 ff.

Peck, *Naga ed-Dêr:* C. N. Peck, *Some Decorated Tombs of the First Intermediate Period at Naga ed-Dêr* (Ann Arbor, 1959)

PM: B. Porter and R. L. B. Moss, *Topographical Bibliography of Ancient Egyptian Hieroglyphic Texts, Reliefs, and Paintings,* vols. I–VII (Oxford, 1927–1951, second edition of vol. I, 1960–1964)

PSBA: Proceedings of the Society of Biblical Archaeology

Rec. de trav.: Recueil de travaux

Reisner, G. A., *Kerma* I–V (*Harvard African Studies* V–VI, Cambridge, Mass., 1923)

Roeder, G., *Hermopolis 1929–1939* (Hildesheim, 1959)

Scamuzzi, E., *Museo Egizio di Torino* (Turin, 1963)

Schenkel, W., *Frühmittelägyptische Studien* (Bonn, 1962)

Servant Statues: J. H. Breasted, Jr., *Egyptian Servant Statues* (Washington, 1948)

Sheikh Said: Norman de G. Davies, *The Rock Tombs of Sheikh Said* (London, 1901)

Smith, W. S., *Country Life in Ancient Egypt* (Museum of Fine Arts Picture Book No. 2)

Smith, W. S., *Interconnections in the Ancient Near East* (New Haven, 1965)

Steckeweh, H., *Die Fürstengräber von Qaw* (Leipzig, 1936)

Stock, H., *Die erste Zwischenzeit Ägyptens* (Rome, 1949)

Wb.: Wörterbuch der aegyptischen Sprache

Winlock, H. E., and Mace, A. C., *The Tomb of Senebtisi at Lisht* (New York, 1916)

BIBLIOGRAPHICAL NOTE

The essential earlier publications of the Djehuty-nekht coffin paintings and the procession of offering bearers are listed here for convenience:

AAAE, pls. 74 B, 75 A, B (paintings) and pp. 107 ff.

Ancient Egypt[4], figs. 50–51, and color reproduction p. 89 (paintings); fig. 58 (procession). Also see earlier editions.

BMFA 39 (1941) 9–10 (procession).

Dows Dunham, "The Tomb of Dehuti-Nekht and His Wife," *BMFA* 19 (1921) 43 ff.

(Illustration of Procession) *JEA* 29 (1943) pl. II. opposite p. 50.

"A Middle Kingdom Painted Coffin," *passim.*

Müller, *Alt-ägyptische Malerei,* fig. 14 (painting).

Müller, "Egyptian Art," pl. 351 (painting).

Servant Statues, pl. 63 (procession).

E. L. B. Terrace, "The Entourage of an Egyptian Governor," *BMFA* 66 (1968) 5–27 (procession).

Also see "A Painting . . . of Hepzefa" and "Paintings . . . at Bersheh," *passim.*

162

NOTES

INTRODUCTION

1. The Djehuty-nekht coffin-text inscriptions are published in A. de Buck, *The Egyptian Coffin Texts,* vols. I–VII (Chicago, 1935–47, OIP 34, 39, 64, 67, 73, 81, 87).
2. *Gr.*³, pp. 170–173. Also Nina de G. Davies and A. Gardiner, *Tomb of Amenemhet* (London, 1915) 79 ff.; C. J. C. Bennett, *JEA* 27 (1941) 77 ff.; R. Faulkner, *JEA* 27 (1941) 166. W. Federn, "Htp (r)dj(w) (n) 'lnpw, zum Verständnis der vor-osirianischen Opferformel," *MDAIK* 16 (1958) 120–130.
3. *JEA* 18 (1932) 33–48.
4. *Ibid.,* p. 34.

THE HISTORY OF BERSHEH

1. See *El Bersheh* II, p. 1 and n. 4. Also H. Gauthier, *Dictionnaire des noms géographiques contenus dans les textes hiéroglyphiques* (Paris, 1925–1929) vol. I, p. 196 (*Wnw*); vol. II, p. 141 (*Pr Ḏḥwty*); vol. IV, p. 176 (*Ḥmnw*). Also P. Montet, *Géographie de l'Égypte ancienne,* 2ᵉ Partie (Paris, 1961) pp. 146–156. Hermopolis has been excavated systematically, if not completely, by Günther Roeder: *Hermopolis 1929–1939* (Hildesheim, 1959), with references to earlier material.
2. G. A. Reisner, *Mycerinus* (Cambridge, Mass., 1931) p. 109 and pls. 38–40; Smith, *OKSP²*, pl. 13 c; Smith, *Ancient Egypt⁴*, fig. 23; Terrace, "A Fragmentary Triad of King Mycerinus," *BMFA* 59 (1961) 41 ff., fig. 4 (new photograph) and elsewhere.
3. R. O. Faulkner. "The Rebellion in the Hare Nome," *JEA* 30 (1944) 61 ff. See also H. Stock, *Die erste Zwischenzeit Ägyptens* (Rome, 1949) pp. 17, 27 (n. 3), 52, 64, 66, 68, 98. The Old Kingdom tombs are published in N. de G. Davies, *The Rock Tombs of Sheikh Said* (London, 1901).
4. The inscriptions in the Hatnub quarries are published in Anthes, *Hatnub.*
5. J. Černý, *Ancient Egyptian Religion* (London, 1952) p. 42. Roeder, "Die Kosmogonie von Hermopolis," *Egyptian Religion* 1 (1933) 1 ff.
6. For Amen at Thebes in The Old Kingdom see now F. Daumas, "L'origine d'Amon à Karnak," *BIFAO* 65 (1967) 201 ff.
7. These will be discussed in such detail as exists in a future volume covering all of the Museum's excavations at Bersheh.
8. The graffito of the reign of Amenhotep III mentioning quarrying for the temple of Hermopolis, observed by Reisner, seems not to have been recorded by him, but its text had been published by Sayce in *PSBA* 9 (1886–87) pl. opposite p. 195; also by Spiegelberg, *Rec. de trav.* 26 (1904) 151–2. The quarries of Nectanebo and probably others are located on the maps in *El Bersheh* II, Pls. II–III. Recent excavations in the plain by the U.A.R. Antiquities Service have uncovered poor burial pits of the New Kingdom, Graeco-Roman and Coptic periods.
9. The 19th-century exploration of the site is recounted in greater detail in *El Bersheh* I, pp. 3–5.
10. *El Bersheh* II, p. 3, n. 1.
11. Daressy, *ASAE* 1 (1900) 17 ff.; Kamal, *ASAE* 2 (1901) 14 ff.; 206 ff.; *ASAE* 3 (1902) 278 ff. See also PM IV, pp. 177–187.

THE BOSTON MUSEUM'S EXCAVATIONS AT BERSHEH

1. Reisner to Lane, February, 3, 1913 (Letter). Letters, diaries, and other manuscript records are preserved in the Museum of Fine Arts, Boston, Department of Egyptian Art. These records are invaluable as documentary data of the excavations of the Department, but are as important for the color they lend to the sometimes dry factual accounts.
2. Reisner to Gray, May 12, 1915 (Letter).

3. G. A. Reisner, *Kerma* I–V (Cambridge, Mass., 1923).

4. *Kerma* IV–V, pl. 31. Smith, *Ancient Egypt*[4], fig. 54, and frequently elsewhere.

5. It is not clear which pits are meant. Daressy and Kamal, both for the Antiquities Service, had made exploratory excavations at the site after the Egypt Exploration Fund excavations. See *ASAE* 1 (1900) 17 ff.; 2 (1901) 14 ff. and 206 ff.; 3 (1902) 278 ff.

6. All these will be published in *The Boston Museum's Excavations at Bersheh*.

7. *El Bersheh* I–II and n. 5 supra.

8. This fact should not be held against Story. He, like others, was taken on by Reisner from the Museum staff, with no previous training in Egyptology.

9. Story to Reisner, May 14, 1915 (Letter).

10. Customarily several gangs of men were at work simultaneously. Thus the Diary entries usually read, e.g., "Thursday, April 29, 38th day. Work on: (1) Tomb 10; (2) Tomb 12; (3) Tomb 13; (4) Front of Tomb of Thuti-hotep." The excerpts quoted here refer only to Tomb 10.

11. This mutilated and unfinished sculpture is apparently the only portrait of Djehuty-nekht preserved to us. I was unable to locate it in the Egyptian Museum, Cairo, where it was apparently deposited. The Expedition number is 15–4–415.

12. Here Reisner was referring to the Cairo Museum. Anticipating that the Cairo Museum would naturally take the coffin of Djehuty-nekht, he was eager to find other objects which he would send back to Boston to justify the Bersheh excursion.

13. For some of the difficulties in interpreting the title *ḥɜty-ꜥ* before the Middle Kingdom, see Peck, *Naga ed-Dêr,* pp. 81–82.

14. E.g. Djehuty-hetep, Newberry No. 2, *El Bersheh* I, pl. VI.

15. See *idem*.

16. cf. Helck, *Beamtentiteln,* p. 57; also *El Bersheh* I, pp. 6–7; Anthes, *Hatnub,* pp. 105 ff.

17. *El Bersheh* I, pl. VI.

18. E.g. *El Bersheh* I, pl. VI; *El Bersheh* II, p. 21, pl. VII.

19. *El Bersheh* II, p. 27, pls. XIII, XV, XVI, XVII, XIX 3, etc.

20. For the genealogies of the Nomarchs at Bersheh see *El Bersheh II, Introduction.* Also see Anthes, *Hatnub* with revisions.

EGYPTIAN TOMB DECORATION AND ITS PURPOSE

1. For this and the following concepts in this section, see Henri Frankfort, *Kingship and the Gods* (Chicago, 1948) and *idem., Ancient Egyptian Religion* (New York, 1948).

2. *BMMA* April 1933 part II 26–27, figs. 5–8, for several of these fantastic creations.

3. Frankfort, *Ancient Egyptian Religion,* p. 101.

4. Frankfort, *Kingship and the Gods,* especially ch. 15.

5. Sir Alan Gardiner, *Egypt of the Pharaohs* (Oxford, 1961), pp. 109–110.

6. In so simple a statement, I have ignored of course such architectural innovations as rock-cut columns, rock-cut vaulted chambers, and the like. It is nevertheless true that these are superficial changes; the basic form of the Egyptian tomb consists of its offering chambers and burial pit. For a survey of the tomb development in the Middle Kingdom see A. Badawy, *A History of Egyptian Architecture, the First Intermediate Period, the Middle Kingdom, and the Second Intermediate Period* (Berkeley and Los Angeles, 1966).

THE COFFINS OF DJEHUTY-NEKHT

1. Smith, *AAAE,* pp. 23 ff.

2. Desheri, CG 1572 = Cairo *Guide* (1966) no. 48; similar chambers also at Sakkarah, C. M. Firth and B. Gunn, *Teti Pyramid Cemeteries* (Cairo, 1926) II, pls. 2–6. Also *ASAE* 55 (1958), part 2, pp. 208 ff., and especially pl. XVII.

3. Cairo CG 28033.

4. Cairo CG 28116.

5. Cairo JE 36445 (Assiut).

6. Cairo CG 28036 where the entire exterior is covered with false door panels. The development of private and royal coffins is outlined in H. E. Winlock and A. C. Mace, *The Tomb of Senebtisi at Lisht* (New York, 1916). It should be noted here that the anthropoid coffin developed also during this period, see *idem.* For coffin development, also see *OKSP*[2] pp. 228 ff.

7. Her inner coffin has been reassembled in the Boston Museum, Acc. No. 21.966.

8. N. M. Davies, *Ancient Egyptian Paintings* (Chicago, 1936) pls. V–VI.

9. Other examples are Paris, Louvre A 23; London, British Museum 30839; Cairo CG 28083, 28085, 28086, 28089, 28091 (see Lacau, *Sarcophages,* pls. LV–LVII). All these coffins are from Bersheh. The Djehuty-nekht map appears in W. S. Smith, *Country Life in Ancient Egypt* (Museum of Fine Arts Picture Book No. 2) fig. 47.

10. *Idem.*

11. Lucas[4] pp. 133–134.

12. *Ancient Egyptian Paintings* III, pp. xxxii–xxxiii.

13. Lucas[4] pp. 339. Also Chapter XIV, *passim.*

14. *Ibid.,* pp. 346–348.

15. *Ibid.,* pp. 340–444.

16. *Ibid.,* pp. 1–2, 3–5, 5–6, 351–353.

17. I am also grateful to Mr. William J. Young and his assistant Miss Florence Whitmore for the great care they went to in analyzing these and other pigments, including original specimens from the Museum's excavations at Kerma. A brief report of some of these pigments is published by Robert E. Ogilvie in *Applications of Science in Examination of Works of Art, Proceedings of the Seminar in 1965* (Boston, 1967); his analysis is made on the basis of the electron microanalyzer.

A SURVEY OF PAINTING IN THE MIDDLE KINGDOM

1. Smith first made this observation on the importance of the breaking up of old usages, their character during the Intermediate Period and the reconsolidation of color in the Middle Kingdom. See *OKSP*[2] ch. XII; "A Middle Kingdom Painted Coffin," p. 268; "Paintings . . . at Bersheh," pp. 321 ff.

2. For discussions of these regional differences, see *OKSP*[2] ch. XII; *Manuel* IV, pp. 48–49.

3. *Manuel* IV, p. 48.

4. G. Jéquier, *Le Monument funéraire du Pepi II,* vols. I–III (Cairo, 1936–1940). *OKSP*[2] pl. 54 c.

5. *Meir* IV, especially pl. XXVI.

6. *Sheikh Said, passim.*

7. PM IV, pp. 134–135. A. Varille, *La tombe de Ni-Ankh-Pepi à Zâoyet el-Mayetin* (= MIFAO 70).

8. *Meir* V, *passim.*

9. *Deir el Gebrawi* I.

10. For the use of curving lines to suggest rounded forms, see *OKSP*[2], figs. 206–209.

11. A drawing of the complete scene is published in Peck, *Naga ed-Dêr* pl. II. The watercolor copy published in our Plate XLVI was made by Norman de Garis Davies and is in the archives of the Department of Egyptian Art, Museum of Fine Arts, Boston. See also *OKSP*[2] p. 223.

12. *Mo'alla, passim.*

13. E.g. the minute pointing of the wig of Kawit, *AAAE,* pl. 61. Also the new Intef, *MDAIK* 20 (1965) pl. XV b.

14. Giulio Farina, *La Pittura Egiziana* (Milan, 1929) pls. XVIII, XX; Ernesto Scamuzzi, *Museo Egizio di Torino* (Turin, 1963) pl. XV; *AAAE,* pl. 58 A.

15. *BMMA* March 1932, part II, fig. 28; *AAAE,* pl. 58 B.

16. *AAAE,* pp. 85–86.

17. Cf. the same subject at Aswan, *Felsengräber,* pl. V.a. In *El Bersheh* II Newberry has wrongly placed the bullfighting scene on pl. XIV; it belongs below the lower scene on pl. XVII.

18. PM IV, p. 263.

19. *Manuel* IV, p. 52.

20. Recently it has been suggested that some of the tombs formerly thought to be of the Eleventh Dynasty should be redated to the early Twelfth Dynasty. See Schenkel, *Frühmittelägyptische Studien,* pp. 78–84.

21. Exactly similar paintings in the nearby chamber of Kemsit are poorly reproduced in color in E. Naville, *The XIth Dynasty Temple at Deir el-Bahari,* vol. III (London, 1913) pls. II–III. The shrines of these ladies, decorated in painted relief are in Naville, vol. II (London, 1910), again in poor color reproductions.

22. For the rise of Theban supremacy, see Hayes, *CAH*[2] vol. I, ch. XX. "The Rise of the Middle Kingdom" (Cambridge, 1961).

23. *BMMA* December 1923, part II, fig. 12 (chamber), fig. 10 (fragment of relief).

24. *AAAE,* p. 86. See *BMMA* March 1932, part II, figs. 25–31 and pp. 32 ff.

25. *MDAIK* 20 (1965) 47 ff. and pls. XI–XX; *MDAIK* 21 (1966) 72 ff. and pls. X–XXII. The excavators, Drs. Arnold and Settgast, kindly allowed me to examine the tomb after the close of their season in 1967.

26. *MDAIK* 20 (1965) fig. 2 (opp. p. 50).

27. Cf. *AAAE,* p. 240.

28. N. de G. Davies, *Five Theban Tombs* (London, 1913) ch. III. A beautifully painted fragment of relief from this tomb (*ibid.,* pl. XLI) is in the Cairo Museum, JE 48848.

29. Cairo Museum 9–12/20–1.

30. N. de G. Davies, *The Tomb of Antefoker* (London, 1920). The tomb is actually that of his wife Senet.

31. Several years ago the Antiquities Service excavated at Mitrahineh (ancient Memphis) several Middle Kingdom burial chambers of mud-brick, lined with limestone blocks. In addition to the usual offering formulae, some of these chambers have painted scenes of daily life including men carrying water, a wine-pressing scene (?), and butchering. The figures are executed on a small scale; the style appears to be rather coarse, however, the preservation is poor.

32. *Meir* I.

33. *Ibid.,* p. 8 and *passim.*

34. Davies, *Antefoker,* pls. VI, VII. For a discussion of the implications of the use of space in these scenes, see H. Groenewegen-Frankfort, *Arrest and Movement* (London, 1951) ch. III.

35. Percy E. Newberry, *Beni Hasan* I (London, 1893) pls. X ff.

36. *Felsengräber,* figs. 10–27.

37. "A Painting . . . of Hepzefa."

38. G. A. Reisner, *Kerma* IV–V, pl. 31.

39. *Meir* II.

40. See Groenewegen-Frankfort, *op. cit.* (supra n. 34). For the latest discussion of the subject of Middle Kingdom painting and relief, and connections with Aegean and Near Eastern art, see W. S. Smith, *Interconnections in the Ancient Near East* (New Haven, 1965) especially pp. 130–154.

41. *Felsengräber,* pls. XXVII ff.

42. *Meir* III.

43. *Beni Hasan* I, pls. XXVII ff.

44. *Meir* VI.

45. *El Bersheh* I. Also see Chapter I of this volume.

46. "Paintings . . . at Bersheh."

47. See nn. 45–46.

48. "Paintings . . . at Bersheh," pl. 21 A.

49. Flinders Petrie, *Antaeopolis* (London, 1930) chapter II and Hans Steckeweh, *Die Fürstengräber von Qaw* (Leipzig, 1936) pp. 30–42.

TECHNICAL APPENDICES

ANALYSIS OF PIGMENTS FROM BERSHEH AND KERMA
by William J. Young *and* Florence E. Whitmore

Pigments from Outer Coffin of Djehuty-nekht

Fifteen small samples of pigment were removed from various places on the coffin, as indicated below. X-ray diffraction analyses were made of these pigments. The samples were centered in Debye-Scherrer X-ray diffraction cameras and X-ray patterns obtained.

1. White: from shield, Pl. XX.

   identified as calcium carbonate.

2. Dark blue: from collar, Pl. XVI.

   identified as Egyptian Blue, copper calcium silicate.

3. Dark Red: from dagger, Pl. XVI.

   found to consist of iron oxide with a mixture of calcium carbonate.

4. Blue: from second block from top left, Pl. XXI.

   identified as Egyptian Blue.

5. Green: from fourth block from top left, Pl. XXI.

   found to be a mixture of Egyptian Blue (calcium copper silicate) and atacamite, a compound of copper chloride, ground very fine.

6. Pink: from vertical stand below arrows, Pl. XIX.

   found to be a mixture of iron oxide and calcium carbonate.

7. Yellow: from third *ḥes*-vase from right in small chest, Pl. XIX.

   identified as arsenic trisulphide (orpiment).

Pigments from Fragment of Coffin 21.816g, Pit 10 A

A. Seven samples of pigments from the painted surface of a wood fragment were analyzed. Each sample was divided into three parts. Permanent microscopic slides were made of the pigments and they were studied microscopically by reflected light and transmitted polarized light.

B. Spectrographic Analysis:

Part Two of the samples was submitted to a spectrographic analysis, Chart I. The samples were inserted in drilled boron-free carbon electrodes; an arc was struck at 150 volts. The spectra of the pigments were made in juxtaposition on the same film which was developed under standard conditions. In order to facilitate the interpretation, a standard sample of Egyptian Blue was included (Sample No. 1, Chart I). The standard sample was obtained from a relief excavated at Amarna (MFA 36.91).

The spectrographic analysis indicated the composition of the pigments as follows:

1. Blue: found to contain a high percentage of copper, silicon, and calcium; with lower percentages of iron, tin, magnesium and aluminum; and traces of titanium.

2. Green: found to contain a high percentage of copper, silicon, calcium; with magnesium and manganese; with lower percentages of iron, tin, aluminum and titanium.

3. Yellow: found to contain a high percentage of arsenic; with lower percentages of calcium and silicon; and minor amounts of magnesium, iron and aluminum (sulphur was not identified in the spectrograph).

167

4. Red: found to contain a high percentage of iron, calcium and magnesium; with lower percentages of silicon and aluminum; and a trace of beryllium.

5. Black: found to contain a high percentage of carbon; with lower percentages of magnesium and silicon.

C. X-ray Diffraction Analysis:

The third samples of pigment were mixed with collodion and positioned on the ends of glass fibers and situated in the center of Debye-Scherrer cameras. The samples were exposed to 35 kilovolts and 15 milliamperes for a period of 4½ hours and X-ray diffraction patterns were made of the samples. On reading the X-ray diffraction patterns and interpreting these patterns with the aid of the ASTM standard index, the pigments were analysed as follows:

1. Blue: Egyptian Blue ($CuO.CaO_4.SiO_2$), artificial frit, a compound of copper, calcium and silica.

2. Green: a mixture of Egyptian Blue, an artificial frit, and the copper chloride compound, atacamite.

3. Red: iron oxide (red ochre, Fe_2O_3).

4. Pink: iron oxide (Fe_2O_3) mixed with calcium carbonate ($CaCo_3$).

5. White: calcium sulphate (gypsum, $CaSO_4$).

6. Black: carbon black (soot).

7. Yellow: arsenic trisulphide (orpiment, As_2S_3).

Painting Technique

Much of the design was first executed in a white pigment of calcium carbonate ($CaCO_3$) in the case of the outer coffin of Djehuty-nekht and calcium sulphate ($CaSO_4$) in the case of the fragment from his wife's coffin. The painting is executed in a tempera technique with the use of either glue size, gum or albumin (white of egg). The actual identification of the tempera medium was not made. The blue pigment corresponds favorably in composition to the copper calcium silicate ($CuO.CaO_4.SiO_2$) which is characteristic of Egyptian Blue. The green is Egyptian Blue mixed with a finer crystalline material that compares favorably with atacamite, a copper chloride compound.

On analysis the yellow pigment proved to be the mineral orpiment (As_2S_3) which contains approximately 51% arsenic and 39% sulphur. Lucas (4th edition, p. 350) knew of its use in Egypt only from the later part of the 18th Dynasty.

Raw Pigments from Kerma

Analyses were made of four stones excavated at Kerma. They were found in debris and are therefore not dated precisely, but belong probably to the Twelfth Dynasty (no. 4) and the Second Intermediate Period (nos. 1–3).

1. Debris K 1603-1607 (14-2-393)

   Red stone identified as hematite with a mixture of quartz.

2. Debris K 1603-1607 (14-2-393)

   A small geode which contained a red pigment; the pigment was identified as hematite.

3. Debris K 1603-1607 (14-2-393)

   Yellow stone identified as yellow ochre (goethite).

4. Debris B 31 (14-3-1383)

   A gray-black stone identified as graphite.

168

CHART I

Spectrographic Analysis of Pigments from Wood Fragment, El Bersheh XII Dynasty 21.816g, Pit 10 A

	Blue	Blue	Green	Red	Black	Yellow
Arsenic, As	ND	ND	ND	ND	ND	VS
Iron, Fe	T/W	W	M	VS	FT	W
Tin, Sn	M/S	W	W	ND	ND	ND
Silicon, Si	VS	VS	VS	M	W	M
Manganese, Mn	F/T	T	W	ND	ND	ND
Magnesium, Mg	M	M/S	S	S	M	M
Aluminum, Al	T	W	M/S	M	T	T
Calcium, Ca	VS	VS	VS	VS	M	S
Copper, Cu	VS	VS	VS	ND	ND	ND
Titanium, Ti	FT	T/W	W/M	ND	ND	ND
Beryllium, Be	ND	ND	ND	T	ND	ND
Carbon, C	M	M	M	S	VS	M
Boron, B	ND	ND	ND	ND	ND	ND
Sodium, Na	W	W	W	ND	ND	ND

KEY:

FT — .001%
T — .001%—.01%
W — .01%—0.1%
M — 0.1%—1%
S — 1%—10%
VS — Above 10%
ND — Not detected

CHART II

Dimensions and Accession Numbers of Outer and Inner Coffins of Djehuty-nekht

Outer Coffin

	Length	Height	Thickness
Head End	1.090 m.	1.030 m.	.165 m.
Foot End	1.140	1.130	.165
Left Side	2.630	1.140	.165
Right Side	2.600	1.160	.165
Lid	2.620	1.140	.177
Bottom	2.440	.965	.114

Inner Coffin

	Length	Height	Thickness
Sides	2.230	.725	.114
Ends	.765	.737	.114

The Museum of Fine Arts Accession Numbers are as follows:

Outer Coffin

Head End	20.1824
Foot End	20.1825
Left Side	20.1822
Right Side	20.1823
Lid	20.1826
Bottom	20.1827

The Inner Coffin is accessioned under one number: 21.962.

INDEX

170

172